MAXIMIZING MEMORY POWER

Using Recall in Business

MAXIMIZING MEMORY POWER

Using Recall in Business

Alan S. Brown

John Wiley & Sons, Inc.
New York • Chichester • Brisbane • Toronto • Singapore

Publisher: Stephen Kippur
Editor: Susan Gies
Managing Editor: Katherine S. Bolster
Editing, Design, & Production: Till & Till

> Wiley books can be used as premiums to promote products or services, for training, or in mail-order catalogs. For information on quantity discounts, please write to the Special Sales Department, John Wiley & Sons, Inc.

Copyright © 1987 by John Wiley & Sons, Inc.

All rights reserved. Published simultaneously in Canada.

Reproduction or translation of any part of this work beyond that permitted by Section 107 or 108 of the 1976 United States Copyright Act without the permission of the copyright owner is unlawful. Requests for permission or further information should be addressed to the Permissions Department, John Wiley & Sons, Inc.

Library of Congress Cataloging-in-Publication Data

Brown, Alan S.
   Maximizing memory power.

   1. Memory. 2. Mnemonics. 3. Businessmen—Psychology.
I. Title.
BF371.B755   1986   153.1'2   86-15813
ISBN 0-471-84721-6 (pbk.)
ISBN 0-471-85405-0

Printed in the United States of America
87 88 10 9 8 7 6 5 4 3 2 1

Contents

INTRODUCTION · vii

WHAT IS MEMORY?

1 Forgetting · 3
2 Memory Stages · 11
3 Memory Styles · 15

THE SYSTEM

4 Attend · 27
5 Associate · 37
6 Rehearse · 44
7 Support · 52

MANAGING YOUR MEMORY

8 Names · 65
9 Personal Information · 87
10 Conversations · 95

11	Reading Material	105
12	Meetings	117
13	Lists	127
14	Tasks to Accomplish	137
15	Tasks Completed	153
16	Numbers	164
17	Making a Speech	180
18	Examinations	186

MANAGING OTHERS' MEMORIES

19	Introducing Yourself	199
20	One-to-One Messages	207
21	Your Audience	213
22	Memos	223

FINISHING TOUCHES

| 23 | Jogging Your Memory | 233 |
| 24 | Making It Work | 243 |

INDEX 253

Introduction

Despite an increased emphasis in the business community on developing sophisticated, marketable talents, one central skill has been ignored—memory management—the ability to learn vital personal and professional material and recall it whenever necessary. The business world presents great information-processing demands. It is necessary to manage a large and complex amount of data in a short period of time. This is the milieu where memory failures are the most embarrassing and costly.

It is possible that memory skills have been neglected because of the mistaken assumption that one is either blessed with a good memory or cursed with a poor one. But memory is a skill that can be improved with proper management. Another reason why memory management has not found effective application in the business community is that few memory experts, who are primarily academics, know enough about the daily obligations and responsibilities of the business executive.

This book stands apart from other memory books in that it addresses the special learning and memory needs of the business professional. For several years, I have tested and refined memory techniques that are of immediate and practical value to the businessperson. From experience gained through a decade of seminar training, consulting, and research, I have revised and refined the basic concepts of memory training so that it best fits the businessperson's special memory needs.

This book is also unique in that it provides a general memory *system*. Other approaches to memory training offer a different technique for each memory problem area: the name-face hook for names, the pegword system for lists of information, the keyword system for numbers. Remembering the techniques is a job in itself! This book teaches a four-step system that can be applied to virtually every type of business information and is both easy to understand and easy to apply. It will increase the efficiency with which you use your memory, and help you appreciate the real benefits that result from a well-managed memory.

A better-managed memory can promote business success. It will save you time—and we all can appreciate the great value of that. Your time is extremely valuable. Unless you have a systematic approach to remembering all the business training you have received, you may be wasting your time.

Not only does it take much longer to learn important information without a memory strategy, but the recall of critical facts and data is more difficult. Learning to manage your memory more efficiently will reduce the drain on time and emotion.

The effectiveness with which you communicate will also increase dramatically with a better-trained memory. Having important names, facts, and business data at your fingertips will make it easier for you to state your case; you will be able to back it up with specifics. In addition, your coworkers will learn to value you as an important business resource—someone to whom they can turn when they need specific information and advice.

Self-confidence is an additional payoff of a well-managed memory. As you apply the techniques presented in this book, you will notice that you come to trust your own memory more and more. You will become more confident in your ability to mentally manage information because you will see that it actually does work.

The first two parts of *Maximizing Memory Power* give you the general principles of memory management. Part one, "What Is Memory?," tells you something about how memory works, how we remember and how we forget. Part Two, "The System," lays out the four-step program I've mentioned—a simple program, applicable to any memory situation, and the framework on which you will build your own memory management.

Introduction

The next two parts, "Managing Your Memory," and "Managing Others' Memories," are the applications of the system, and are divided into specific situations. Perhaps you won't need to deal equally with each one of these. You may have no trouble at all remembering names, for instance, or tasks you have to perform. On the other hand, you may not do at all well with reading material or in meetings. Here is where you make your individual choices; select the chapters that you feel will help you most; scan the others, or if you are absolutely certain that you need no help at all in some areas, skip over these.

The fifth part, "Finishing Touches," provides practical tips on how to get information out when your recall efforts temporarily become ineffective, and how to change your habits to make improved memory management a reality.

Don't be unrealistic in your expectations. Your memory will not miraculously improve immediately. You are already managing your memory, but you are probably not doing it as well as you should. In learning better memory techniques, you will be fighting old habits. The temporary conflict between the new and old habits will make progress slower at first. Concentrate on two or three specific points until you can see some real improvement. Then undertake a few more challenges. You will find that as the memory management skills become stronger and more a part of your daily life, the rate of improvement will increase.

You won't find stories here of stupendous feats of memory. The aim is not to make you into talk show performers, Mr. (or Ms.) Memory Whiz. Stories like these are irrelevant in a book whose readers want improved everyday memory skills, and will only daunt the reader. I don't want to scare you, but rather coax you gradually into applying improved management skills.

This book's primary purpose is to provide an easily understood and readily applied system for work-related memory difficulties. It is *not* a compilation of scientific studies in which each point is documented and I impress you with the breadth of my scientific knowledge. I have extracted the essence of research findings and presented it to you in a form that you can apply to your own life. Finally, the book is *not* a collection of memory tricks, gimmicks, or party demonstrations. There are other books available for this.

Each chapter has applications beyond the business realm: your church, civic, social, and recreational activities can all benefit. Once you get into the habit of better memory management in business, it will automatically enhance your personal life as well. After all, your memory works the same way after office hours as it does during them.

Your memory can be improved, and the more you work at it, the better it gets. It never wears out, it is never used up, and you always have it with you for quick reference. A sharpened memory can improve your creativity, imagination, problem-solving skills, and communication ability.

An Invitation

Knowledge is an ever-growing, ever-expanding endeavor. Too often, a book like this is seen as an intellectual end product. I would like to assume that this book can initiate new dimensions of understanding and application concerning memory. If the book does that, it is successful.

I invite you to participate in this ongoing research in the laboratory of the real world. As you apply the suggestions and ideas in this book, keep track of your experiences. Let me know what works best for you, and what additional discoveries you make along the way. What improvements or embellishments would be useful? Do you have interesting or instructive stories concerning your memory?

Please write to me with your comments, concerns, or stories:

Dr. Alan S. Brown
Department of Psychology
Southern Methodist University
Dallas, Texas 75275

Acknowledgments

Permission to quote from the following sources is gratefully acknowledged:

The quotation on page 14 is reprinted from *Improving Your Memory* by Laird S. Cermak, by permission of W.W. Norton & Company, Inc. Copyright © 1975 by W.W. Norton & Company, New York, New York.

Quotations on pages 46, 159, and 237 are reprinted from *Techniques for Efficient Remembering* by Donald A. Laird and Elanor Laird, by permission of McGraw-Hill Book Company. Copyright © 1960 by McGraw-Hill Book Company, New York, New York.

The quotation on page 67 is reprinted from "It Pays to Remember Names" by James McMahon in *Supervision*, Vol. 44, No. 2, March 1982, by permission of The National Research Bureau, Inc., 424 North Third Street, Burlington, Iowa.

The quotation on page 165 is reprinted from "That Filing System Inside Your Head" by Roy Rowan in *Fortune*, August 28, 1978, by permission of *Fortune* magazine.

WHAT IS MEMORY?

To get a solid foundation on which to build new memory skills, you must understand the different aspects of memory:

Forgetting: Why, and in what ways, does memory fail?
Memory Stages: The three successive steps through which information passes on its way to being stored permanently:

- Sensory memory
- Short-term memory
- Long-term memory

Memory styles: The different ways different people perceive and remember their experiences:

- Visual
- Auditory
- Motion

1

Forgetting

"I'd forget my head if it wasn't attached to my neck," goes the old saying. As it is, too many of us forget the name of a colleague or client, can't remember what the boss's spouse looks like, can't tell without looking at the committee report whether the cost of the new project will be $27,000 or $37,000. Why? There are three possible basic reasons:

- The information may have been deposited in your long-term memory, but gotten mixed up with other memories, or faded away because it was not strengthened sufficiently by rehearsal.
- The information is still there, but you can't pull it out at the moment. Ever had a name on the tip of your tongue? Memory is formed and stored, and unless you have a "tip-of-the-tongue" problem, you pull it out when you need it.
- Of course, if the information never got in to begin with, you haven't really forgotten it. You simply didn't hear the name, or notice where you set your briefcase.

Why does this happen? The causes of forgetting can be broadly grouped either as psychological or physical.

☞ PSYCHOLOGICAL FACTORS

At the present time, hundreds of researchers in dozens of countries are actively pursuing the causes of (and cures for) memory lapses. Their work bears out the belief that most of the causes are not physical, but psychological. Below are some of the causes of forgetting that their research has turned up. Some are necessary and beneficial, but others just keep us from enjoying an effective memory.

Natural Housecleaning

Consider, for a moment, all the information you take in during a typical day. You meet new people, find out about new products, learn what the weather will be, hear the latest about two employees in another department who are having a running conflict.

In your typical day, you probably experience at least fifty items of information of varying degrees of importance to you. If you saved all this information in your memory forever, you would find yourself with an unmanageable stockpile of data and facts. Think of a short-order cook who automatically remembered all his previous orders!

Luckily, we have a memory that is like a self-cleaning oven. It continuously works to thin out the unnecessary contents of our mind so that we can more easily find what we need when we need it. In order to store information permanently, we have to repeat or rehearse it within a certain period of time after receiving it. If we don't, it is likely to fade away.

Have you ever thought it would be wonderful to be able to remember everything you experienced? It's not. A person with a photographic memory often finds it more of an annoyance than a blessing. Images keep popping up in a disordered and confusing fashion. One memory triggers another, and then that triggers another. Any experience can start an avalanche of memories tumbling out.

Protection

Another function of forgetting relates to experiences we have had that are dangerous, emotional, or otherwise traumatic. When something extremely unpleasant happens, our memory may protect us from the agony of reliving the experience by simply erasing it or making it inaccessible.

People seriously injured in a car accident commonly blot out the memory of the last minute before the crash. This memory gap is an aid to psychological recovery; it helps keep the traumatic experience from interfering with the work of returning to emotional health.

Stress

We all know that stress can be physically devastating. It can have considerable negative impact on memory function as well.

Executive stress can put a double whammy on your memory. First, it can hamper your efforts to store new information. When you're under stress, there is an enormous expenditure of psychological energy on worry, fear, and anxiety. This can be either specific (Can I finish the Watson contract on time?) or general (I'm slipping in my job skills and can't seem to keep up). In both cases, we use psychological resources nonproductively, and they are then not available for capturing and storing the information in memory.

Second, stress can block access to information already stored in memory. Have you ever been talking in front of a group and suddenly gone blank? You can barely remember your own name, much less what the last point you made was, or where you are heading. This memory lapse also occasionally occurs during introductions. People may "block" on a friend's name at the moment of introduction.

Are there certain situations in which you seem to lose access to well-learned information, for example:

Talking to the boss?
Addressing the department?
Lecturing an errant employee?
Making introductions?

You are stressed—nervous about the forthcoming situation. You may become short of breath or dizzy; you may yawn or be unable to concentrate. When you experience one of these symptoms, try one of these quick relaxers:

1. Take a few deep breaths and let them out slowly.
2. Close your eyes, clear your mind of thoughts, and generate a peaceful scene to concentrate on.
3. Alternately tense and relax your shoulder and neck muscles several times.

These are only a few of many techniques for relaxing, and there are many books available for more specific instructions.

Context Change

As you sit at your desk writing, your pen runs out of ink. Searching your drawer, you find that you are out of ballpoint pens. Walking down the hall to the supply closet, you stop for a minute to chat with Fran. When you reach the closet, you stare inside blankly with no idea why you went there. You wander back to your office, plop behind your desk, and it jumps back to you—you need another pen!

When you have a thought or learn something new, the place where you experience it, the external context, often becomes linked with the memory and becomes a powerful cue to help recall it. When you are in that same place again, recall of the earlier thought is easy, but when you are in a different place, recall of that idea is sometimes difficult.

We see most of our acquaintances in a consistent location: the microcomputer salesperson always comes to our office and the mailroom clerk is in the mailroom. When we run into one of these people at the hardware store, it is often difficult to recall his or her name.

Context-specific forgetting is one of those difficulties that you have to put up with. Derive some comfort from knowing that it is normal and happens to all of us. There is, however, one technique to help reduce these "context" effects. Practice recalling the persons you have learned when you are in different locations. Retrieve the name (and face) of the mailclerk, the secretary, and the salesperson when you are at home or at the grocery store. As you indirectly experience them in different places, you induce some degree of retrieval flexibility for all names you memorize.

Completion

At the start of the day, you have five projects ahead of you. During the day, you spend an hour and a half on each task. You complete three tasks and assume that you will not encounter them again. For the other two projects, you have to wait for an OK from the purchasing agent, and she is out sick. You can't get an answer on when she will be back to work—maybe tomorrow, maybe by the first of next week. When you return to work the next day, you are more likely to have forgotten your *completed* tasks than the incompleted ones. This is a way your memory can work more efficiently, by clearing out some details that you don't need to deal with any longer.

Denial

In our lives, there are a number of major and minor annoyances that plague us. These difficult situations can sometimes be sidestepped conveniently by forgetting about them. You get a letter from the IRS asking for more information about your charitable deduction to the New World Church, a tax break your accountant suggested. After putting the letter aside, it slips your mind until the reminder letter arrives from the IRS a month later.

An obnoxious customer calls and asks you for an explanation why his order is late. You are in the middle of something now, and promise to get back to him in an hour. But you forget completely to phone him—and you get an even nastier call from this customer the next morning.

In these examples, the forgetting served as a temporary psychological salve against facing an uncomfortable situation. The best protection against denial is to face the realities immediately. If an employee is suspected of stealing, deal with him or her as soon as possible. The more quickly you confront the painful task, the less likely you are to "forget" it until you have compounded the difficulty.

Avoidance

While denial pertains to specific incidents, avoidance covers broader topics such as meeting people, paperwork, dealing with numbers, or with money. I have found that some people who claim to have difficulty with names are really shy people, and that the name "difficulty" is an accommodation to their shyness. It gives them an excuse not to deal with people, since they cannot remember them.

A colleague I know attends departmental meetings regularly, but has little recollection the next day of the issues covered in the discussions. After repeated complaints, it became clear to me why: He hated the meetings, thought they were a waste of time, and felt forced to attend. By forgetting what had been accomplished, he confirmed to himself that the meetings were as he saw them—pointless.

Attention from Others

We all care about other people, and want and need a certain amount of attention from them. Unfortunately, some people use forgetfulness as a device to gain attention. Others chide them. Friends tell teasing stories about their memory mishaps.

Be careful. If you derive some social benefit from your memory difficulties, your pleasure in that benefit may sabotage your efforts to improve your memory.

Laziness

Another psychological block to memory improvement is laziness. The key to improving your memory is the desire to do so. If you cannot see the value in memorizing names, information, and numbers, you probably won't make the effort.

Do you have any special memory problems that may be serving a special psychological function? You'll have trouble improving your memory in that area if your "weak" memory is directly tied to a basic need or fear.

Forgetting

👉 PHYSICAL FACTORS

Because the memory is part of the brain, a number of physical and chemical traumas to that organ can impair one's ability to learn and to recall information.

Alcohol

"Every time you have a drink, you destroy a thousand brain cells!" I have been given this "fact" numerous times, and asked nervously whether my questioner is doing permanent damage to learning and memory ability by consuming alcohol. Even if this dire prediction were true, which it probably is not, a quick calculation reveals that it would take several million drinks to kill off all the neurons in one person's head! Alcohol in moderation does not appear to impair memory function, but research indicates that consistent "binge" drinking could affect your memory.

A more common alcohol-related difficulty is that when you have had several drinks, you may have difficulty remembering a piece of information that you learned when you were sober. The opposite can also occur, where you learn something during a cocktail party which you have difficulty remembering when you are sober. The memory is usually still there, but it is more difficult to get at momentarily because of a changed mental state. This is similar to the changed-context difficulty under psychological factors.

Nutrition and Exercise

The brain is an oxygen hog. It accounts for about 2 percent of the total body weight, but consumes 25 percent of the oxygen! Anything that restricts the flow of blood will have a major impact on the brain, and on memory efficiency. Clogged arteries, whether from poor diet or lack of exercise, will contribute to reduced efficiency. You won't necessarily lose specific memories, but you may find general difficulties in learning and in recalling information.

At the present time, there is scant evidence that specific vitamins, minerals, or exotic foods will enhance memory function.

Stroke and Head Trauma

Even a minor stroke or head injury can damage parts of the brain where memories may be stored. A recent research article reported on a head trauma patient whose memory was fine—except for the names of fruits and vegetables! A personal friend recently suffered a mild concussion in a car accident. After several weeks, all her memory functions seemed to be intact except spelling. She would have great difficulty with words she formerly knew quite well, and would have to depend on a trial-and-error procedure for generating the correct spellings.

If you start experiencing difficulty in one isolated function of memory, head trauma (undetected stroke) might be the cause, and a physical checkup is indicated.

Aging

The common belief that senility and memory loss are inescapable consequences of the aging process is generally untrue. Research indicates that older adults who remain mentally active (reading, thinking, solving problems) show little or no decline in memory efficiency. In fact, some of these old people had better memories than the average college-age student.

The elderly may have the *same* number actual memory lapses as young adults, but it simply causes them greater concern because it is associated in their minds with "losing it."

One age-related condition which *can* cause severe memory difficulties is Alzheimer's disease. This disease's initial, and most pronounced, symptom is difficulty in retrieving names for objects. Alzheimer's disease causes you to forget the names of *common* objects such as a toothbrush or a light bulb. Anyone who is experiencing this difficulty consistently should seek medical help.

2

Memory Stages

Memory is not monolithic, although most of us think of it that way. Actually you have *three* different types of memories:

- *Sensory*, which briefly holds sensory impressions
- *Short term*, which puts a memory into some form that is relevant to the individual
- *Long term*, where the adjusted impression is stored permanently

When people discuss memory, they are usually referring to long-term memory.

Compare these basic memory processes to writing a story for a newspaper. A reporter gathers pertinent facts by visiting the locale of the event, taking pictures, recording statements from key individuals, and making various personal observations. The amount of potential information is enormous, and the reporter must be skilled both at gathering a variety of different types of data and deftly discarding the information that is not needed. This process corresponds to *sensory* memory.

The reporter then takes the collection of facts back to the office to be organized, modified, edited, and made more understandable to the eventual reader. The more relevant a fact is, the better able the reporter will be to remember it. The process of putting information in a form that can be remembered more effectively is the function of *short-term* memory.

Our reporter finally prints out a copy of the story, which is then recorded on newsprint. The published paper corresponds to *long-term* memory: both permanently store information that can be retained and consulted on a continuing basis.

☞ SENSORY MEMORY

Your senses are automatically and continuously gathering information, even though you may not immediately be aware of it. Tune into your senses for a moment: smell, touch, sight, and sound. You are seeing this page, hearing various background noises, touching the book. You may be smelling perfume or coffee.

Most of this information is held only briefly, for a second or two. The information important to you at the moment quickly moves on into your short-term memory for further deliberate processing. The rest is discarded.

Visual information is passed along because you are reading. Right now, that is foremost, while information about sounds or touch is probably dropped because it isn't relevant. You do monitor those other sense channels, however, like an automatic security system. If information appears that is strong or unusual or personal—your name being spoken, the smell of smoke, or an itchy foot—your attention will be captured by it momentarily. But most of the time, you consciously select which sense to focus on, letting information to the other senses quickly fade away. All too often, the environment may dictate the focus of our attention. But by applying the suggestions in this book, you can learn to be master of your sensory information input.

Of course, in order to take in information and process it into short- and long-term memory, we must be receptive to it. A lack of attention to sensory impressions, "daydreaming," concentration on some other subject, leads us to miss what is being presented to us by our senses.

When there are too many distractions or too many things to pay attention to at one time, you will also lose information. Have you ever tried to listen to an explanation of an employee's work while being interrupted three times by your phone and twice by your secretary? In this situation, it's nearly impossible to transfer pertinent information to short-term memory because it has already disappeared, falling out of the trapdoor of sensory memory.

Memory Stages

☞ SHORT-TERM MEMORY

After you successfully capture the information and send it to short-term memory, you must convert the new information (name, fact, date) to a "familiar" form which can be easily filed in long-term memory. Think of it this way: A librarian takes time to classify a new book so that it fits in a logical way with the books already there. Otherwise, it would be nearly impossible to find.

In the same manner, you put new information in a logical format to make it easier to find later. You store a new company policy on travel along with what you already know about the subject. A person's name is converted into some image impression (visual, auditory, or motion) which you are most comfortable with. An important phone number is personalized by a particular number coding which you use.

Short-term memory is often called "working" memory. In less than a minute, you carry out a delicate balancing act: you hold on to the information so it doesn't fade away, but quickly put it in a form compatible with your own storage of experiences and data in long-term memory.

If too much information is balanced at once, something may get bumped out and lost forever. We can work on a maximum of about seven or eight pieces of information at once in this memory before risking loss and confusion. A local seven-digit phone number is readily manageable, but a ten-digit long-distance number exceeds your short-term capacity. Holding the long-distance number from the phone book through your completed dial sequence may be a challenge.

The short-term memory has another function besides digesting incoming information. It helps retrieve information stored already, as well as monitor our current thoughts and decisions. Short-term memory controls input, output, and current operations. In a sense, it is like the control tower in a busy airport—directing incoming flights to the correct runway, routing outgoing flights in the proper direction, and organizing the movements of planes on the ground.

Because the short-term store is limited, it can most efficiently aid in memorizing new information if not preoccupied with extraneous thoughts or retrieval requests. If you have ever missed somebody's name because you were worried about an incompleted project, or missed what the boss was saying because a colleague asked you who won the 1982 Super Bowl, you have experienced short-term memory overload. Capacity was used up and didn't allow room for additional incoming data.

☞ LONG-TERM MEMORY

There are billions of nerve cells, called neurons, in the brain. Each one is capable of thousands of connections with other brain cells, allowing a nearly unlimited number of possible connections. It is these connections that make up long-term memory. Because there are such an enormous number of them, the long-term memory has virtually unlimited capacity.

"You can store ten memories a second for your lifetime and only use up half the brain's capabilities." "You only use 10 percent of your brain's capacity." Scientists writing about the brain are fond of statements like these. The fact is that we simply don't understand enough about how memories are formed. But what we do know, and what all professionals in the field agree on, is that we use only a small fraction of our total memory capacity.

Nor do we store permanently *all* the information placed in long-term memory. For some reason, new memories tend to fade over the first few hours and days in long-term memory, unless we recall and refresh them periodically.

Just think of the potential of this unlimited long-term memory—a bodily function that cannot be overloaded and that won't wear out from excessive use. In fact, it seems that the more you use long-term memory, the more efficient it gets!

> It is believed that the more information there is in long-term memory, the easier, not harder, it is to get more information in; because the more you know, the more complete your organization system is and the faster you can catalogue new information (Laird S. Cermak, *Improving Your Memory*).

3

Memory Styles

There appear to be fundamental differences in the way different people perceive and remember the world. While we all pass information through the three basic memory stages—sensory, short-term, and long-term memory—there are differences in the *type* of information that the individual is most sensitive to, or tuned into. These differences appear to show up early in life, and have an important impact on how we experience our world, remember it, and communicate these experiences to others.

A self-assessment scale is presented on pages 15–17. For each statement, select *one* of the three alternatives that most closely suits your personal preference or behavior, and put a checkmark in front of it. (Letters following statements will be used for scoring.)

For some items, none of the alternatives will fit *exactly* what you would do in that situation. Pick the *best* option from among the three. Don't try to second-guess what the "right" answers are—there are none. Also try to avoid "what is done" in your profession or your company, school, or family when taking the test. Answer in a way that feels right for you, personally.

I get the most out of information when it is presented in:
_____ c. trial runs
_____ a. graphs
_____ b. conferences

If I have a problem to solve, my first impulse is to:
_____ b. gather advice from others
_____ c. conduct an on-site investigation
_____ a. read current information about that type of problem

When learning about a new concept, I absorb it quickest when I can:
 _____ a. read a booklet
 _____ b. attend a good lecture
 _____ c. do a run-through

To get feedback from someone about an idea, I am most likely to say:
 _____ b. "How does this sound?"
 _____ a. "Can you picture this?"
 _____ c. "Let me run this by you."

I derive the most enjoyment in exploring new topics by:
 _____ a. reading a description
 _____ c. having it demonstrated
 _____ b. hearing someone explain it

When saying good-bye to a friend, I am most likely to say:
 _____ b. "Talk to you later."
 _____ c. "I'll be in touch."
 _____ a. "See you soon."

If I need to provide a detailed explanation to someone, I prefer to:
 _____ b. engage in direct dialogue
 _____ a. write it down for them
 _____ c. show them

I am most likely to be kept awake at night by:
 _____ c. an uncomfortable bed
 _____ b. a dripping faucet
 _____ a. a light on in the room

I can most easily tell when people are nervous by:
 _____ b. listening to their voice
 _____ c. noting their body posture and movements
 _____ a. looking at their facial expressions

In analyzing a new procedure, I find it most helpful to:
 _____ a. draw a diagram
 _____ c. run through the steps
 _____ b. talk about it

I am most easily distracted by:
 _____ a. objects that are disordered or out of place
 _____ b. loud or unusual noises
 _____ c. sudden or erratic movements around me

Complex data are most easily summarized in:
 _____ c. a working model
 _____ a. a table
 _____ b. a descriptive story or narrative

Scoring. Referring to the letters beside each alternative, count the number of times you checked *a, b,* and *c* and record this beside these totals:

---

a. _____   b. _____   c. _____

Let's hold off discussing the test results for a few pages. I want you to read the following section without being biased by the test results.

In the next part of this chapter, I will describe three types of memory functioning. As you read the descriptions, think about how closely each one applies to you.

☞ MEMORY MODES

Most of what we experience comes to us through five basic sensory "channels"—sight, sound, touch, smell, and taste (smell and taste do not play a major role in day-to-day memory requirements and will not be covered any further here).

Just as people differ in their preference for types of music or food, they differ in which sensory mode they prefer. Some people are most attentive to what they see; thus they remember visual information very well. Others readily retain what they hear. And some people best remember events, movements, or what they actually did.

My position is that sight, sound, and the physical action we perceive by touch, which we call kinetic or motor, are three primary types of memory, all potentially equal in clarity, impact, and value. Most people use all three sensory modalities, but the relative effectiveness of the modes differs from person to person. Although some individuals experience themselves as primarily visual, auditory, or motion, most people experience their strongest form of memory as a combination of two modes, such as visual-auditory, motor-visual, or auditory-motor. Often, what stands out most clearly in peoples' minds is what mode they are *weakest* in.

In the next three sections, descriptions are presented for each of the three memory modes: visual, auditory, and motion. These are general descriptions which contain all the characteristics of that memory channel. Although interest in these individual differences has intrigued memory scientists for over a century, laboratory research has been minimal. The descriptions presented in this chapter are primarily a result of my personal observations and assessments of individuals over the last decade of teaching, training, and research.

As you read through each description, determine how well it describes the way you approach the world. After you finish all three, you should have a clear idea of your own memory pattern and what your most effective memory strategy should be.

Visual Modality

If you are a visual person, you respond well to written communications—memos, letters, reports, and outlines. Because you remember these messages best, you prefer to send written documents for coworkers to digest. Mental pictures help you understand complex policies or plans. When someone tells you about a flood of paperwork, you may automatically "see" in your mind a river of paper coming toward you. As you hear about interest rates dropping, you may generate a graph in your head which shows a line curving downward. Words pop almost effortlessly into images and mental scenes. You sprinkle your language with visual images:

"What does this *look* like to you?"
"Can you *picture* this?"
"That's a good *illustration* of the point."
"The new plan requires a thorough *examination*."
"The problem just became *clear* to me."
"He has shown a *pattern* of irresponsibility."

During a presentation, you respond best to diagrams and

graphs. *Seeing* how various parts of a plan are connected with each other is essential. If someone is discussing an idea or project, you may prefer to have an outline in front of you for reference. Without an outline or agenda, you may drift off, become confused, or focus on other things. During a conversation, you like to generate or write down points as they are made to get a handle on what is being said to you. When a work problem arises, your first impulse may be to read about the solutions or to consult the directions, user's manual, or records. You have faith that written documentation will provide complete answers and solutions.

Visual disorganization may be disorienting or distracting to you. Your work area is probably well organized. If you have to deal with a lot of paperwork, you will attempt to classify it, file it, and maybe create homogeneous piles. You pick up on the visual organization of a room that you enter, and have a good memory for objects and color schemes. You probably have a good sense of direction and do not often get lost. To remember a route, you tend to focus on physical landmarks.

Auditory Modality

If you are an auditory type, you remember verbal communications well, whether they are heard over the phone, on a recorded message, or through direct, face-to-face encounters. You have an exceptional memory for distinct phrases, songs, poems, or catchy slogans. Although everyone is attracted by unusual messages in advertisements, you will grasp them immediately and find them bouncing around in your head. Because oral messages are so easy to remember, you prefer to use informal discussions or phone calls to convey important information. You will often find yourself saying things aloud to clarify and remember them. Talking things over to yourself, both out loud and in your head, is a common experience. This is a technique you use to make sense of and remember your experiences. The auditory style may work its way into your speech in phrases such as:

> "Let's *hear* them out."
> "Something *sounds* funny about that."

"We need to *tune in* to what's going on."
"I have to *confess* that I don't understand it."
"This is a very *telling* message."
"We should *consult* with an expert."
"As I *hear* it, we should go ahead with it."

During a meeting or presentation, your natural focus is on catch phrases and vocal emphasis used by the speaker. You can remember entire sentences verbatim. You can detect whether the speaker is nervous, excited, or possibly not telling the truth through the tone, volume, and texture of his or her voice. If a difficulty arises at work, you will initially seek advice from others. A book on the subject will be useful only if you can discuss it with someone. Writing memos or letters is difficult for you; it is much more satisfying to pick up the phone and call someone directly. Toll-free 800 numbers and hot-lines are important sources of information to you.

Auditory people are unusually sensitive to background noises. The ticking clock or dripping faucet will grab your attention and distract you. If the background noise is melodic, soothing, or familiar, such as radio music or low-level conversation, it may provide a good working background for you. On the other hand, harsh, irregular, or mechanical noises will make it difficult for you to perform efficiently.

Motion Modality

If you are a motor-oriented person, you are especially sensitive to your own movements and the motion of objects and people around you. You like to touch and hold objects, and walk through the steps of a process. Communication is most effective through demonstrating. Hand gestures make a good substitute for direct demonstration. Since touch is important to you, you will often touch those to whom you are talking. It is a way for you to gather extra information from your companion, just as the auditory person gathers information from what and how something is said. In a routine conversation, you may feel a need to walk with your associate while the two of you talk. Being able to pace back and forth will help you think things over. You will naturally attend to and remember the movements, body posture, and particular gestures of others. Your memory style may be evident in your use of words, with such phrases as:

"We need to *move* on this."
"It will be a miracle if we *pull* this off!"
"I *feel* there is a problem."
"Something about it *strikes* me as peculiar."
"That idea will have a large *impact*."
"Let's *push* forward on the plan."
"This will *shake up* the competition."

Motion is important to you in keeping your learning and memory channels "open," so it is difficult for you to sit still for too long in a meeting or conference. The most memorable format for work plans and projects involves a time line or a flowchart. Both of these show a sequence of activities through time and space, and the implication of motion in a two-dimensional drawing is easy for you to relate to and remember. Tying the information into specific events or experiences, whether in the future or the past, is important. If you run into difficulties at work, you are likely to trace back through the steps, take the object apart, or try to think of what was done in the past.

You are sensitive to background motion around you. If the flow is orderly and predictable, it provides a good working environment. On the other hand, erratic, sudden, or unusual movements are distracting and take attention away from the task at hand. You are receptive to being touched when talked to, but do not like to be bumped or pushed. You are exceptionally good at remembering the details of an event, such as when it occurred, who was involved, and what they did. On the other hand, you may not remember clearly what the participants said or looked like.

☞ YOUR PERSONAL MEMORY STYLE ASSESSMENT

Now that you have read through the three profiles, you should have a better idea of your own memory pattern. Take a moment to rank your own self-assessed style by putting an *S* beside your strongest mode and a *W* beside your weakest one.

_____ visual   _____ auditory   _____ motion

Now refer back to the test you took to determine how your personal assessment matches the test results. In the test scoring, *a* is visual, *b* is auditory, and *c* is motion. The highest number should represent your strongest mode and the lowest your weakest mode.

Your own assessment should match up with the test. If it doesn't, carefully observe your own behaviors and preferences for a while. You don't have to settle on your particular memory style at this point in order to benefit from the remainder of the book.

☞ MEMORY MANAGEMENT USING MEMORY STYLES

Identify Your Strong Modes

Many people think that the sense they use most often in their job is their strongest one. This may not be the case. Individuals often find themselves in positions where the requirements do not suit their memory styles but they view themselves as having the strength the job requires because they use it so often. Switchboard operators whose auditory mode is relatively weak may assess themselves as strong auditory individuals because hearing is such an integral part of their occupation. A repair technician may assess motion as his primary mode because of the activity required by the job. A graphic designer may feel that she is mainly visual because the work demands approaching each project that way.

Think about what you remember most easily, or what is the most enjoyable learning situation for you. When you go on a vacation, what memories do you bring back with you: the scenery and settings that you saw, the activities that you participated in, or the sounds and voices that you heard? When you meet someone, do you remember the face and clothing, the voice quality, or the handshake and body movements?

Once you are certain what your strongest memory modality is, you should always try to direct information to it. If you are strongly visual, express experiences and ideas visibly through sketches, drawings, or written documents. In the business setting, use charts, diagrams, and pictures. If you are auditory, direct important information to your sense of hearing through talk or music. In a business context, engage in conversations, attend lectures, or listen to tapes. If you are motion-oriented, involve body movement in your learning process. When learning a task, walk through each of the steps or put the parts together for yourself.

In the applications chapters (sections Three and Four), numerous concrete examples are provided on how to translate experiences into each modal format, to make them more memorable.

Involve Additional Senses

Another way to sharpen remembering is to expand your learning experiences to involve senses besides your strongest one. Experiencing information through an additional sense builds another "path" to help guide you to the information later. After experiencing something in one channel, use other senses to enrich that memory.

You will often find yourself in a situation which fits a memory style other than your preferred one. A clear understanding of the memory styles will enable you to manage the situation better. For instance, an auditory person may need to use some visual strategies to remember faces better. Or a motion person could benefit from hearing techniques to improve memory for conversations. A visualizer could use a motion approach to enhance his or her memory for a production sequence.

Cushion Your Weaker Senses

Learning to identify those situations that make demands on your weakest sense is critical to improving your memory through being aware of your memory style. Do you find your attention drifting during conversations or lectures? Perhaps sound is your weakest mode. Do you become confused or distracted when someone demonstrates the use of a new office machine? Maybe your weakest mode is motion. Do you tune out if a number of charts and diagrams are presented during a meeting? Then it could be that sight is your weakest mode. In these situations, make an extra effort to pay closer attention, or direct the information to your stronger sense to make it more memorable.

EXERCISE
Reflect back on your experiences for the last day or two. What things stand out—sounds, sights, or activities?

Do you have a consistent communication difficulty with a friend, a coworker, a spouse, or a supervisor? Is it possible that this person's memory mode pattern is different from yours? Pay careful attention to what he or she says or does over several days. Be especially aware of any evidence of what sensory mode this individual prefers. Perhaps communication problems exist because the two of you are processing information in different ways.

THE SYSTEM

This section of the book presents a simple, four-step system for effective memory management. The system is built on the memory principles described in the first section. When it has been thoroughly described, the system will be applied to specific areas of memory problems. The four basic steps are

Attend: Get a clear and immediate hold on the information.
Associate: Translate the information into a personalized form.
Rehearse: Strengthen the information through repetition.
Support: Supplement your memory through external aids.

You will find these steps repeated each time we deal with another area of memory. Think of it as a drill that helps you to use the system and to apply it to new situations with ease.

None of these four steps is new to you. You already use them every day in your efforts to remember people, facts, numbers, events, and experiences. In the next four chapters, you will learn how to use each of these processes **more effectively**.

The purpose of the system is **not** to create a "whiz kid" memory. What you need are specific, concrete suggestions that can help you better remember your experiences. Select specific parts of the system to work on. The improvement in your memory should be immediate, motivating you to select additional strategies to continue the strengthening of your memory.

As with any type of behavior change, memory improvement works best in small steps. When you want to get your body in shape, you don't begin with eighty push-ups. You begin with short, relatively easy exercises, building your muscles gradually through repeated, ever increasing sets of exercises. Improvement in memory management should be approached in the same manner. Select a few procedures to practice, use them until they are automatic, and then add a few more. In a short time, you will enjoy the benefits that improved memory management can yield.

4

Attend

A business associate calls you at your office, and asks about a project on which you both have been working. After you have been talking for several minutes, your eye catches a piece of unfinished work on your desk. Your mind drifts away from the conversation for a few moments. Suddenly, you are aware that your attention has wandered and you pull yourself back to the conversation. At that point, the other person asks your opinion of something he just said. You are caught in an embarrassing situation. Do you admit that you drifted off and excuse yourself, or try to cover up and fake a response?

Most of us have found ourselves in such a situation. In "What Is Memory?" I noted that all information must first pass through sensory memory, a very efficient recording device that holds an exact copy of the material for a few seconds. This is where our attention mechanism does its work—selecting the appropriate information from sensory memory to pass along to short-term memory for further processing. A great deal of information is "lost" because it was never transferred into short-term memory in the first place.

We are in the habit of ignoring most of the sensations we receive. Our ears are picking up sounds as we read the newspaper, but the sounds are ignored because we don't need them. Our eyes capture information from our desk as we talk on the phone, but this information drops away immediately; like most of the information we receive, it is not important at the moment.

Being selective is fine; the crucial question is, what do we choose to select? What are we noticing that we should be ignoring, and vice versa? How often have you left your home and not been able to remember whether you locked your door, or turned off the stove? You probably did it, but you have the habit of ignoring routine behaviors, because often what is going on inside your head is more interesting than the tasks you are performing. People occasionally drive on the open rode for several miles, caught up in their own thoughts, and are suddenly shaken because they've forgotten to make the turn that will get them to their destination. Even complicated actions can be carried out without your attention—or *any* awareness.

This habit of inattention can become a problem when you find yourself focusing on nonproductive events (worrying about meeting your sales quota) while missing important ones (the sales meeting you are sitting in now). Try to catch yourself as soon as your mind wanders. It may be pleasurable in the short run to let your thoughts drift off. Remaining attentive can be hard work. But it can pay off in improved memory. After all, if you can't get the event into your short-term memory, you don't have any chance of remembering it.

EXERCISE

How well do you pay attention? Try these simple questions.

1. What color is the upholstery of your car?
2. In what direction does Lincoln face on the penny?
3. What was the most recent thing your boss said to you?
4. What two letters are missing from a telephone dial?
5. Does your wristwatch have arabic, Roman, or no numerals?

If you answered all five questions correctly, your habit of attention is very sharp already. If you missed any, read the Attend sections in Parts Three and Four with special care.

☞ IMPROVING YOUR ATTENTION

My belief is that poor attention is the greatest problem in memory. Most of the memory difficulties I have observed can be traced directly to not getting the information in the first place. If you have nothing to work with at the start, storing it in long-term memory is impossible.

Your overall goals for improved attention should involve spending less time in your own thoughts and finding a way to make your experiences more interesting, intense, and personal so they will attract and hold your attention better. The following are a number of specific suggestions for achieving the goal of better attention.

Familiarize Yourself with the Subject

Have you noticed that when you buy a new make of car, everyone else suddenly seems to own one? Or after you start an IRA, dozens of articles about IRAs appear in the newspapers and magazines? Actually, the world has not changed. You have simply begun paying attention to things you ignored before. Your new knowledge and experience have opened your sensory awareness.

Put this idea to work for you. Learn more about the tasks you have to do or the projects to which you are assigned. If you are interviewing a candidate for a job, study his or her credentials ahead of time. If you are going to a meeting, request an agenda before you go, so that you will know what to focus on while you are there. The better informed you are ahead of time, the easier it is to pay attention to and *remember* your experiences. It is like tilling your mental soil so the seeds of memory can grow more easily.

If memory for names is a problem, get a book about the background of names and read up on the various meanings. If remembering numbers is always difficult, get an elementary book about the history of our number system. A few hours of reading can initiate a new area of interest, making attention and memory easier.

Make the Experience Personal

Attention is automatically alerted by items that are personally relevant. While talking with somebody at a party, your attention will be snatched away if you hear your name spoken across the room. While idly flipping through a magazine, your attention will be captured when the name of your company flashes by on one of the pages.

Think about the last business meeting at which your mind kept drifting away. Despite shifting in your chair or stretching, you lost the struggle. Chances are you saw no personal relevance in what was being said. What holds your interest in a good novel or short story? You can imagine yourself, or someone you know, in it. It is important to you—you can relate it to your own life and experiences.

Nearly any experience can be made relevant to you in some way. Discover what dimension of the information relates to your current or past activities. Imagine a way in which it could apply to you in the future. Is there a friend or associate who is interested in the area, with whom you could share the information?

Learning about steel output in the People's Republic of China during 1981 may seem totally irrelevant to your personal life. But you could relate it to your football interest (Pittsburgh Steelers), your Chinese neighbor, or what you were "producing" in 1981 to make it easier to attend to.

Intensify the Sensory Impact

Your attention will wander if the sensory stimulation becomes too monotonous or invariant. If you have listened to a salesman drone on about his product or punched numbers endlessly into the calculator, it may become impossible to maintain attention on that activity. Your senses desperately seek stimulation from other sources, just to keep you awake!

To keep your attention focused on the present task, make the sensory impact more intense or varied. Sit closer to the speaker at the luncheon, turn up the volume on the taped message, or make an enlarged copy of a small or detailed diagram.

Besides exaggerating the message intensity, try translating it into another sense. Intensify the impact by absorbing it through several different senses. When grappling with a multipage memo, read it out loud. While talking with a business associate, jot down notes to add visual input.

Use Competition

Many people enjoy competing against other individuals, groups, time, or just themselves. If (and *only* if) you are this type of person, try some of the following techniques.

When confronted with a situation in which it is critical that you learn a lot of material or in which concentration is important, try competing as a way to rivet your attention to the material. In this case, you are competing against time. Divide the material into sections and set a time in which to learn the first section. Then the second, and so on, adjusting the allotted times as you discover what is realistic and what is not.

If you are attending a seminar, make a bet with your colleague that you can learn more participants' names and companies than he or she can—loser buys lunch. This, of course, assumes that your colleague is also energized by competition. You will both benefit not only by paying closer attention to information, but by getting extra rehearsals (see pages 44–51) as you later show each other what you have recalled.

Remember spelling bees in elementary school? If your company or work group is fairly loose and informal, why not try an adult version? Suppose that there is a new policy manual that must be memorized, or the fall product line has just come out and all employees need to know the items forward and backward. After everyone has had sufficient time to learn the material, divide into two or three teams and develop a quiz question format, along the lines of a television show. The team getting the most correct answers receives some sort of prize or trophy.

Make a Cost–Benefit Memory Analysis

Motivation to remember can help to open the front-end memory gate—attention. As with any task you encounter, there are certain costs of forgetting and benefits connected with remembering. Take an area where you feel a need for improvement and carefully assess the pluses and minuses connected with memory.

If remembering what you read is your problem area, make a detailed analysis of the advantages of improved memory for in-house reports: quicker recall of company facts; ability to impress colleagues; dealing more efficiently with inquiries from customers. Now list the negatives of poor reading memory: feeling foolish when called upon by your boss; reading the same report twice; looking stupid with a client when you don't appear to know your facts. Use these good and bad consequences to help focus your attentional efforts. Striving to achieve the reward and avoid the difficulty can hold your attention on target.

Physically Prepare Yourself for Remembering

There are steps you can take to prepare yourself for situations in which you will have to remember a lot of material. We all have daily cycles of alertness. Some of us are morning people, some get charged up in the afternoon, and the rest of us become energized in the evening. If you have to manage some information during one of your "off" times, when your energy level is low, get a cup of coffee, do some deep breathing exercises, or jog up a short flight of stairs to keep you alert enough to be attentive.

Another key to physical preparation is taking a short break between different activities. If you have a meeting to go to or a conference with an employee, pause for a few moments to collect your thoughts, and mentally redirect your memory efforts to a different activity.

When you need to meet new people, arrive early at the conference or party. As one of the first persons there, you will have plenty of time to absorb each person's name as he or she arrives. More important, you won't have to suffer through the introduction blitz—meeting two dozen people at once as you walk in the door.

Avoid Self-Talk

Everyone daydreams from time to time. But when your mind is tied up too often with imaginary situations, information from the senses does not get through. If the habit of self-talk has become excessive, and you are losing substantial information because of it, remedy this by making a *conscious* effort to attend to everything you do: talk about or comment on it; touch it; make a mental note of the colors and textures. A small amount of time spent in training your memory to focus outward will pay off in greater powers of awareness and retention.

To help avoid daydreaming and self-reflection while you should be paying attention to current experience, set aside one specific *location* (your work desk, for example) and *time* during the day (say 11:30 to 11:45 in the morning) and make that your daydreaming period. If you reserve a time and place for reflective activity, you may be less likely to engage in it off and on during the rest of the day, where it will disrupt important incoming information.

EXERCISE
If you spend an excessive amount of time inside your own head, try this retraining exercise. Set a wristwatch or calculator alarm (which can handle short periods) or a timer for twenty minutes. When it goes off, record whether you were paying attention to the outside world or to your own thoughts. If you were attending to your internal world at the alarm, repeat this cycle. Set the alarm for another twenty minutes and make a determined effort to keep focusing on the outside world. Keep doing this until you are consistently attending to what is going on around, not inside, you.

Avoid Self-Consciousness

Another hinderance to one's attention is self-consciousness. This is a negative form of self-talk usually involving worry or concern: How do I look? Did she take my comments in the right way? When you are focused on yourself, you lose the ability to gather data from the world around you.

One especially disruptive form of self-consciousness often takes over when you are being introduced. You are so concerned about how you look (Did I comb my hair?) or sound (Did I say the right thing?) or come across to a future business associate (Does he think I'm competent?) that the name often slips by. Regardless of how sharp you look or how competent you sound, if you forget the other person's name, you will not have made a favorable impression.

Keep Environmental Distractions to a Minimum

A magician makes a living by distracting you to take your attention away from what he is really doing. By tricking you into looking at the wrong hand, he makes you miss the switch.

The work environment can be full of routine business distractions, making it difficult to pay attention to even important information. If your mind continually drifts away during phone conversations or you lose track of what's being said in the middle of a report, your office environment may have too much noise, excess clutter, or continual movement. Become aware of your own sensitivity to different types of distractions. To improve your concentration and memory ability, remove the disturbances, or remove yourself to another work area.

Find the Right Level to Begin At

Some information may be so complex that you may have difficulty remembering it after your first encounter with it: a computer operator's manual, or the instructions for a supplemental tax schedule. In many cases, complicated material does not register with you because you cannot pay attention long enough to figure it out. This difficulty can be avoided by breaking the information down into several levels of complexity and tackling each level before learning the next one.

An acquaintance bought a home computer, but the manual that came with it was too complex. Rather than putting him into the computer age, it put him to sleep. He became discouraged and put the entire project aside. A year later, he stumbled across a book that presented the information at a clearer, more elementary level. After learning this information successfully, he went back to the more complex book and learned from it. Building up your understanding in progressively more complex levels enables you to maintain attention more easily.

Don't Juggle Too Much at Once

A hard lesson for most of us is the limit on how much information we can handle at once. People differ considerably in how many things they can simultaneously attend to. All of us have had things "slip through the cracks" because our attention was too consumed with other activities. Become aware of what your personal limits are, and try to plan your day to stay within them.

On those occasions where you become aware that you did lose track of an activity (I forgot to call Joan back about the contract!), stop immediately and write down *all* the tasks you are engaged in at the moment. After several of these episodes, you may get a feel for how many tasks are *too* many for you, and you can deliberately cut back on the number in the future to avoid this problem.

Finish a Task before Going On

As you may recall from Chapter 1, "Forgetting," projects or tasks that are incomplete tend to stay on our minds until we finish them. So if something is left unfinished, it will consume a part of your working short-term memory capacity, and keep you from tracking and remembering present activities.

Of course, if it is important to remember completed tasks, you can "fool" your memory by making them artificially incomplete. For instance, don't fill out the last of the paperwork on important tasks until the end of each week. This way, some memory trace may linger for a few days, and be more likely to etch a place in your long-term memory store.

But if this is not the case, try to finish whatever task you are working on before tackling another one. This is especially true when you encounter intense memory demands, such as an important policymaking meeting or an interview for a new vice president.

Approach your tasks one at a time. Trying to juggle several at once will often deter you from paying full attention to any.

EXERCISE
Here is a quick test. Circle YES or NO for each question.

YES   NO   Do you ever notice small bruises or cuts on your body, and not remember how you got them?

YES   NO   Do you often ask people to repeat what they have said?

YES   NO   Do you repeatedly misplace small items such as keys or glasses?

YES   NO   Does your mind wander while reading a magazine or newspaper article on a subject that interests you?

YES   NO   Do you occasionally drive several miles before you suddenly "snap awake" and realize you have no recall of the last few miles?

If you answered YES to two or more of these questions, you may have a serious inattention habit. Make a special effort to apply the attention-improving tips provided later in this book.

5

Associate

You are in a conference with your boss, in which she is explaining the upcoming efforts to cut expenses. As she launches into one of her important cost-cutting plans, a clever idea occurs to you. Not wanting to appear impolite and interrupt, you hold on to your suggestion until she stops talking. After she finishes her point, you realize that you have forgotten what you wanted to say.

Has something like this happened to you? Your idea was captured and stored for a moment or two, but was not packaged into a quick association to store it in memory. There was additional material coming into short-term memory that bumped out your suggestion.

The task of association is to convert the information into a personally usable form. You have "captured" the information in your sensory memory and passed it to your short-term memory. As in a manufacturing process, the raw material must be shaped into a usable product. It must be put in a form for effective storage in long-term memory.

Forming associations is similar to personalizing the new information—relating it to people, things, words, events, or ideas that you already know. This is similar to managing the information flow in a business. Once a customer's order is called in, it is put on the proper forms (associate) and directed to the proper department (storage area). If the appropriate forms are *not* filled out, the order may get routed to the wrong department or be lost. Memory works much the same way. New information must be linked with what we already know and understand in order to be effectively remembered.

Created associations should be considered as memory catalysts. They help to establish memories quickly and clearly, and may drop away as the memory becomes stronger with repeated use. You don't use association aids to remember your parents' names, your hometown, or the name of your company. However, to remember a decision made in Tuesday's meeting or the name of the new secretary, associations are of great assistance.

☞ TYPES OF ASSOCIATIONS

In this section, a number of different association techniques will be introduced and related to one of the three sensory modalities: visual, auditory, and motion. If you are a visual-motion person, you will probably understand and relate best to suggestions in the visual and motion sections. However, you should not ignore the section on auditory associations. Become well acquainted with all three types because specific situations may arise that require an association strategy other than your preferred one.

☞ VISUAL

Real Visual Representations

"Sight persons" can often remember actual visual information in a remarkably detailed manner. These persons can see, in their minds, a printed page where they saw a particular office policy or a name printed on somebody's name tag.

Abstract ideas or complex business procedures should be written on paper, with key points capitalized, underlined, highlighted in color, or written in different styles. Names can be printed on makeshift name tags or written in a list. The route to a client's office should be drawn out as a map. You'll remember organizational structure best if you make a comprehensive chart of it, with hierarchical levels and accountability precisely detailed in the location of each job box and the length of lines between them. Actual photographs and sketches can often make a complete memory imprint for visual persons.

Created Visual Images

Although "seeing" actual information is ideal, many situations do not lend themselves to this. When listening to someone or driving a car, it may be impossible to create actual visual records of the information.

In these cases, use mental pictures as a substitute. Close your eyes for a moment, and form a mental picture of your car. Visually minded persons will find this easy because they are so used to doing it, while others may take more time to create the imaginary picture. Your car is an actual object, but with a little effort you can create images of your own design, such as a six-foot green carrot lounging in a hammock. Even though you have never actually seen this (I hope), you can construct the picture in your mind.

You probably do this when a stranger is described to you, or when talking to someone new on the phone, or listening to someone on the radio. You generate a picture of what you think the person looks like. When meeting that person later face to face, you are occasionally startled because your generated image does not match the reality.

Create mental images that are unusual or distinct. Think about the things that naturally catch your eye—colorful, large, unusually shaped, or completely unique objects. The more extraordinary it is, the more distinct an impression it makes and the easier it is to remember. Your "mental eye" works the same way. If you want to remember to get an estimate from Hartford Body Shop, imagine your car smashed into a large red heart. If you want to remember Fred Williams, think of a last *will* and testament being *fried* to a golden brown in a skillet. The picture of a fried will should remind you of Fred Williams.

As you practice creating these mental pictures, they become easier to generate. Close your eyes while making these images, if this helps (unless you are driving), so that you won't be distracted by real objects around you. The mental picture does not have to duplicate exactly the thing you must remember. Part of the information is usually sufficient to trigger the entire memory, as with our friend Fred Williams.

☞ AUDITORY

Actual Sounds

Auditory persons are often skilled at holding their actual sound experiences in long-term memory, like an extensive audiotape library. They can remember hearing someone say a particular statement, or listening to a recorded message, or even saying something aloud to themselves.

Auditory individuals focus on the distinctiveness in the sound of voices and rhymes, and establish that rhythm in their mind to remember the information. Saying out loud the information to be remembered—a report or the name of a company—while reading it is helpful. Saying it in an unusual tone of voice or with an odd stress pattern is even better for forming a memory. An auditory person can say a new name or term out loud, putting the stress on the wrong syllable, repeating it very loudly, putting it in a falsetto voice, or speaking very slowly or rapidly. Using a make-believe voice makes the memory more distinct. For instance, if you repeat a customer's name in a voice that mimics Humphrey Bogart's (not to the customer's face, of course) makes the impression much easier to remember.

Imagery with Stories or Phrases

Another auditory association method is generating a story, a short poem, or a catchy phrase. To remember the essence of a long memo, a sound-sensitive person can generate several short phrases and repeat them. There are a number of common auditory aids in the form of rhymes that are used by almost everyone: "Thirty days hath September, April, June, and November," "*I* before *E* except after *C*," or "Every good boy does fine" for the lines in the treble clef. Advertisers are also aware of the impact of melody, rhythm, and rhyme in creating a radio or television message that will be remembered.

These phrases do not have to be grammatically proper, and the poems do not have to be eloquent with perfect meter and rhyme. They work best if they are unusual, with contrived words or slang expressions. To remember that Cross Industries will now be headed by David Chadwick, one could say, "David is not cross, just a tad sick." The phone number 552-2000 could be remembered by saying, "Double five, double two, zips."

Acronyms are also useful for those with an auditory memory. In an acronym, you create a word from the initial letters of the words in a list. To remember to get pencils, rubberbands, erasers, and paperclips from the supply closet, think of the word "prep."

☞ MOTION

Firsthand Experience

For persons sensitive to motion, "being there" is an important ingredient in memory. If a new communications system is being considered for the office and the motion-oriented individual wants to learn about its operation, actually visiting a location to witness it in use would make learning about it much easier.

Three-dimensional models are helpful because they simulate the physical aspects of the object. Films and videotapes can be useful associational devices; they allow vicarious participation in the experience. The strongest motor memory is one that activates the entire body; for example, wandering through the various departments of a company to better understand the organization's workings. Imagining movements is also useful in building associations. As someone gives verbal directions, the motion person can imagine driving the route.

A flowchart is another way to establish a motion association because it moves or flows through time in a sequence of steps, from left to right or top to bottom. For the same reason, the movement involved in the use of flip charts can help form distinct memory associations. A progressive slide show, which builds step by step, contains associational motion.

Although the end product is visual, the act of writing something down is an effective motor aid to association because of the movements of the arm and the hand. Some motor persons even write notes and then throw them away—simply writing the information down was sufficient to fix it in memory.

Relating to Prior Experiences

Another motion technique involves connecting new material with prior events or experiences. When learning a new name, one might imagine a connection between the new person and an acquaintance. When introduced to Tom Baxter, link this person to another friend named Tom.

When encountering a new procedure, movement-sensitive individuals should relate it to one they already know or understand, emphasizing the similarities and differences. A new company name can be linked to a similar one: Thompson Electronics can be connected with Thompson Dairy, and Criswell Office Supplies can be related to the other two suppliers, BRG and Warner. The names can be experienced as "stacked" on each other, linked by a chain, or bumping into each other, creating the type of mental motion or activity that is important for the motion-oriented person. Although this may seem partly visual, it is the *activity* that is the essential ingredient for the motor memory.

☞ GOOD ASSOCIATION HABITS

Allow Plenty of Time to Form Associations

Each new piece of information that enters short-term memory must have an adequate amount of time devoted to it to allow effective association to be created and stored away. When too many pieces of information are experienced at once, the limits of your short-term memory may be violated, with the resultant loss of some information.

As you practice, you will become faster at forming associations and this will reduce your limitation. But you should remain sensitive to situations in which information is presented too rapidly, and figure out ways to avoid it.

Avoid Multiple, Interfering Associations

When too many similar or conflicting associations are learned, they can interfere with or block each other. Most people have experienced occasional confusion when meeting two people with the same first or last name—was Charles Baxter or Charles Thompson the sales representative? When a friend moves residences, the new phone number can become mixed up with the old one.

There are occasions in which two different names or products or ideas that are too similar to each other are difficult to keep apart. Your mind tends to blend them together. Try to learn the agents from First Equity Bankshares at a different time from the representatives of First Indemnity Brokers. When you have the possibility of confusion, make a special effort to create very distinct associations to keep the similar information from getting mixed up.

Avoid Too Much Passive Information

Watching television can create poor memory habits. Television is a passive medium; the information is presented in a way that limits your involvement. You are not encouraged to handle and remember complex ideas, or conjure up images and solve problems. This takes the keen edge off your ability to associate, because the information is presented in a predigested form. You don't even have to figure out what is funny or not—the laugh tracks will do this for you.

If you do watch television, select the more complex and challenging programs. Try to substitute a stimulating conversation or reading a controversial book as an alternative to television. This will put a sharper edge on your mental abilities.

EXERCISE

Consider a recent situation where you had to remember something: a name, an address, or a phone number. What type of association technique did you use? Was it visual, auditory, or motion, or some combination?

After reading this chapter, can you think of anything that you could have done to enhance your memory of it?

6

Rehearse

You receive a memo from your department head about an upcoming meeting with a candidate for the job of field manager. The area to be headed is a critical one. You mark the date and time on your calendar and review the woman's name several times until you are sure that you have it set in your mind. Then you throw away the memo, comfortable that you "have it down." On the day of the meeting, you enter your boss's office to come face to face with the candidate—and you can't recall her name. As you stare, and then try to fake it until someone says the name you're looking for, you can't believe that it slipped your mind.

Have you found yourself in this uncomfortable situation on occasion? You try to fix some information in your mind, like a date or a name, only to find later that you have no idea what it was. And then you blame your bad memory, rather than blaming the real culprit—*ineffective rehearsal*.

Nearly everyone thinks they know what rehearsal is. In school, you assumed that the best way to learn new information was by reciting it over and over again. If you had a poem to remember, you recited it many times to get it "fixed" in memory. Remember the elementary school teachers who make their students write on the blackboard "I will not talk during class" fifty times, assuming this will ensure that the student learns the lesson? This type of parroting, or rote repetition, works well for acquiring physical skills such as playing the drums or riding a bicycle, but it is not very efficient for information memory. As with many common beliefs about memory, there is considerable misunderstanding and misapplication of rehearsal techniques.

Rehearsal is a way to solidify information in permanent, long-term storage. Strangely enough, once an association has been formed, it is not automatically guaranteed a permanent seat in long-term memory. New memories must be periodically revived and refreshed after they are first formed, or they will slowly fade away.

Rehearsal is like getting a new office policy established. You can't say it just once—you have to send three memos, announce it in two successive weekly meetings, and then post notices in twenty key locations. Only then does it become permanent policy.

☞ INCREASING YOUR REHEARSAL EFFICIENCY

Review Immediately after the Experience

The point where a new memory is the most fragile is immediately after it is formed. No other repetition will be as important as the one that comes just after you experience the new information. Grab some time after every new experience to reflect on it. Pause for a minute after reading an article to rehash it. Spend five minutes after a meeting going over the points that were discussed.

Space Out Later Rehearsals

The most effective rehearsals are spread out, rather than bunched together. Researchers have consistently found that separating rehearsals over a period of time results in much stronger memory.

Not only should you spread out your reviews, but for the optimal results you should progressively increase the length of time between successive rehearsals. The strength of a newly formed memory association decreases rapidly at first, and the rate of decline then gradually slows down. The graph on the next page illustrates this on the bottom line. This is what would happen without rehearsals.

To counteract this dropoff, the memory needs to be bolstered more often at the beginning, less often later on. If you learn a new name over lunch one day, rehearse it again after you get back to the

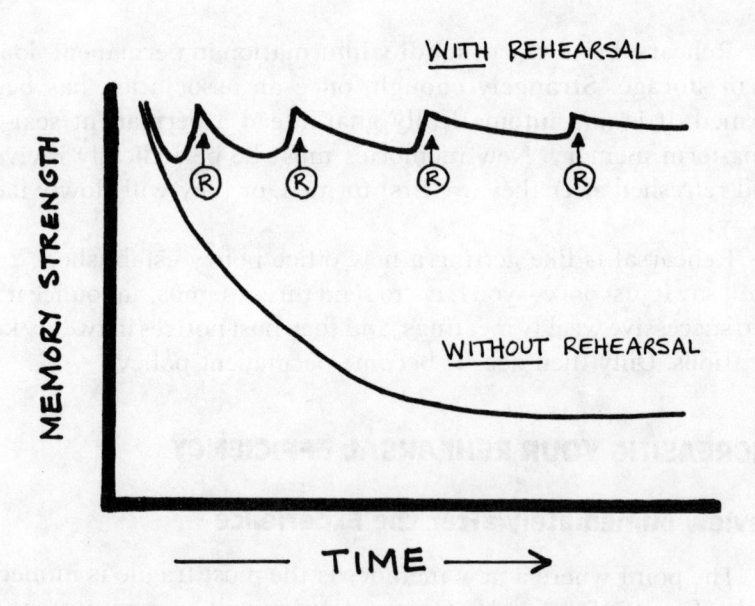

A graph comparing memory strength over time, WITH REHEARSAL (with R points marking rehearsal moments that boost memory strength) versus WITHOUT REHEARSAL (showing steady decay).

A comparison of memory strength changes with and without extra rehearsals

office, on your way home that evening, before you go to bed that night, during the next evening, and finally that weekend.

> Dr. Sarah D. McAustin compared the results from rereading technical material five times in one day, with reading it once a day for five days. A month after reading, those who had reread it five times in one day...recalled 11 percent...but those who had spread out the rereading over five days could recall 30 percent of the material (Donald and Elanor Laird, *Techniques for Efficient Remembering*).

Create Daily and Weekly Reflection Times

A number of businesspeople have established rehearsal breaks as a regular part of their daily activity. Several times each day, usually before lunch and before leaving the office, they rehearse new information. It takes only several minutes to reflect back on the day's activities and to bring up any freshly formed associations. These people are often surprised at how much information will pop back to mind, information they had almost lost.

A weekly rehearsal pause can also be beneficial. The two most effective times are on Friday afternoon and on Sunday afternoon.

The advantage of Friday is that the events, information, and data are still fresh. But it may be a time of interruptions, fatigue, and distractions. Sunday afternoon is a more relaxed and unhurried period to engage in memory rehearsals, but you may have lost some information from the prior week by then. Allow ten to fifteen minutes for reflection time, because when you ponder your experiences, it takes a little time to pull all the information out. So don't rush it.

Quiz Yourself

One danger with rehearsals is that they can become boring. When you rehearse some data, pull them back out of memory, jazz them up a bit, and become reinvolved with them. If you fail to pay *active* attention while you rehearse, you won't necessarily lose the information but it may not become any stronger.

One way to make rehearsals more interesting and effective is to ask questions and answer them. What four main points were contained in that memo? What were the two investment law changes mentioned in the meeting this morning? Questions are doubly effective rehearsals, because you must think through the material to come up with the question in the first place, and then again to generate an answer. This technique also provides a quick check on what is missing from memory by noting the questions you could not answer.

Use a Discussion Partner

Another way to make rehearsals more interesting is to talk about the material with someone else. This way, you get two repetitions: the other person's comments and your own. Discussions with another person yield the additional benefit of checking the accuracy of your memory. We often color our associations with our own biases, and comparing our own memory with another person's recollection can eliminate these mental distortions.

While engaged in dialogues, avoid formulating what you are going to say next while the other person is talking. Listen earnestly, and this will strengthen your memory for the material. Ask questions about information, even though you may already know the answer. It helps to hear the same information over again.

Put It into Different Sense Channels

Another way to put some pizzazz into rehearsals is to duplicate the information in another sensory mode: if your hear it, write it down; if you see it, say it to yourself. Although you may be an auditory person and receive information best by hearing it, you can gain extra memory benefit by repeating it through writing or doing. The more senses involved, the more complete the memory.

The most effective rehearsals are those that duplicate the information in the manner in which you will have to recall it. If you are given a telephone number, for example, practice punching it on a phone. Punch in the numbers a few times without lifting the receiver. You will most likely have to say names out loud, so if you learn a new name, say it over and over to yourself.

State It Another Way

State the information in a different way, or try shortening or paraphrasing it. If you receive a letter from a client, condense it into two or three meaningful sentences. After a planning meeting, put the four new policies in a shortened version of your own words. When you finish talking with a coworker, write down the three or four decisions that were made.

With each rehearsal, do not attempt to duplicate the information exactly. Get the gist of it and rehearse that. It is rarely essential that you remember something verbatim, anyway.

Try some additional techniques to get a different angle on it:

- Describe it to an imaginary friend.
- Compare it with something you know.
- Define it, dictionary style.
- Find arguments for or against it.
- Organize it into several different categories.
- Determine how it could change your life.

Review in Different Settings

The goal of improved association and rehearsal techniques is to create a memory that is easily accessible; one that you can recall on the spot with little effort. When memories are formed in a particular setting, and rehearsed in only that setting, it may be difficult to recall the information in a different place. The colleague whom you always see in a particular office becomes difficult to place when you bump into her at the shopping mall.

To help avoid this difficulty, repeat what you have learned in a variety of different locations. If you learn it in the office, repeat it on the way home. For material learned at a conference, rehearse it at your office.

Put It on Tape

A portable cassette or microcassette recorder/player can be useful for rehearsals. The time during recreation, exercise, or commuting can be made productive with a tape playback system. When you are learning new names, lists, or the contents of a booklet, record the important information on tape and play it back during these periods when there are not so many "information-processing demands" on you.

Record the names of new customer leads as you get them and play back the list when driving home from work. While walking from the bus to your office, play back the summary made after you read the report the night before. You can also use tape players to rehearse information while jogging, sitting in a spa, biking, working out with weights, or walking.

Pay Attention to Your Rehearsals

Have you ever, at a party, met a person with an unusual name? You made a special effort to remember it—you repeated it to yourself four or five times. Were you surprised when you could not remember it just fifteen minutes later?

Repeating material without actively paying attention to it does little to improve the strength of the memory. People adapt very quickly to, and ignore, something repeated over and over again. You have heard the seat belt buzzer in your car so often that it has lost its meaning—it is simply something that happens when you turn on your ignition.

Don't let rehearsals go the way of the seat belt buzzer. Force yourself to pay attention to the rehearsals by making them fresh and interesting. Techniques will be provided in Parts Three and Four to help accomplish this.

Rehearse Even "Simple" Items

You meet John Smith at a business club meeting, and think to yourself that this name can be instantly remembered because it is so common. So you don't give it a second thought. The next day, you want to give him a call but are amazed to discover that you have lost his name. What you *do* remember is that it was simple—Jim Brown, Bill Johnson, John Smith?

Beware of thinking that you don't need to rehearse information that seems simple and straightforward. Regardless of how easy the information appears to be, it requires adequate rehearsal to be stored effectively in memory. Even simple names, obvious titles, or clear conclusions need rehearsal. Actually, simple things may need *more* rehearsal because they are more easily interfered with by other common facts, names, or ideas that you already know.

Overrehearse the Information

Whenever you rehearse information, it may seem logical to stop when you feel that you have it down cold. But rehearsing information *beyond* the point where you think that it is well learned (overlearning) can actually be beneficial. Research has shown that these extra rehearsals will make the memory more quickly accessible and less likely to be lost or disrupted through interference or stress. If you want extra memory protection, then overrehearse the material.

EXERCISE
In what situations do you make a special point of rehearsing new information?
List the types of rehearsal techniques you presently use and rate their effectiveness:

Rehearse 51

	How Effective?		
Rehearsal Technique	VERY	SOMEWHAT	NOT

1. _____ _____ _____ _____
2. _____ _____ _____ _____
3. _____ _____ _____ _____
4. _____ _____ _____ _____

What can you do to improve your less-effective rehearsal efforts?

7

Support

You return to your office after a long and productive business conference with a client, in which you laid out the general framework for a three-year project. As you reflect back on your conversation, you cannot remember whether you set up a time next week to talk more about the plan, or whether you only discussed the possibility and left it up in the air. Checking your appointment book, you do not find any entry but you still cannot be sure because sometimes you forget to mark down appointments.

Do you sometimes find yourself at the mercy of an inefficiently used reminder system? Sometimes you use it and sometimes you don't. You have this difficulty because you are mismanaging your *memory supports*.

You are confronted with a great deal of information in a single day. Much of it is trivial and can be discarded almost immediately, like junk mail. But managing the rest requires some skill and attention. Most of the information that you receive falls into one of the following categories:

1. *Immediately forgettable information.* Is it raining outside? Is Mary in her office? This type of information is useful for a moment or two. It can help you make short-range decisions, but has little or no long-range value. Therefore, there is no need to remember it.

2. *Long-term information: immediate access.* The name of your boss's spouse, the new access code for the computer, and your social security number all have two things in common: They are important, and you should have the data immediately recallable. It is not good enough to have the name of the boss's spouse written in a

notebook somewhere. You need to have it accessible at all times. Much of this book presents techniques to improve your ability to form associations and strengthen them in order to make such memories permanent and easily accessible.

Immediately forgettable and long-term (immediate access) actually represent the extremes of information. The following types fall in a gray area somewhere between these extremes:

3. *Long-term information: delayed access.* As with category 2, this involves information that needs to be permanently stored. The difference is that you don't have to produce it on the spot. Your coworkers' birthdays or the number of shares of stock you own are types of information that you can comfortably store outside your brain, rather than committing to memory. Being caught not knowing how many shares of stock you own is not going to embarrass you or make you look incompetent.

4. *Temporary information.* You must call a client in Los Angeles at 4 P.M., or get a proposal in the mail today. These are examples of temporary information: items you must remember for a short period of time, but can forget when they are completed. In order to manage this type of information, it is *not* necessary to form solid associations and carry through systematic rehearsals.

An important part of successful memory management is acknowledging that there is some information that must be stored inside your head and some that can be available externally. Management of information in categories 3 and 4 will be covered in this chapter. Once important information is in your short-term memory, you must make a quick decision: Do I need to store this mentally so as to have it at my fingertips, or can I store it externally, through some kind of support technique?

The use of external memory supports is occasionally viewed as a poor substitute for memorization. If you have to resort to external memory aids, you may be lazy or stupid. Nobody could consider Einstein stupid, and yet he relied on supports for even simple things such as his own phone number. Why memorize it, he figured, if he knew where to quickly locate it? Although this may be an extreme position, it suggests that smart persons are adept at discriminating what should be memorized from what should be supported.

The use of external support methods has a long and distinguished history. Books and scrolls were actually developed as a memory support for the oral tradition of storytelling. Songs and ceremonies were originally created to externally record the tribal history. Some early churches hung dead bodies around the sanctuary as an external memory support, to remind the congregation of their own mortality.

Memory support techniques can be an invaluable aid to a busy person. When applied properly, they can be more effective and dependable than mental storage of the facts. Research has shown that over a lifetime, a person values and uses this type of memory aid to an increasing degree. In fact, many elderly people have developed a surprising repertoire of external memory backups that help them manage their daily routines successfully.

In modern times, we use a variety of memory supports. In our cars, we have the gas guage, the seat belt buzzer, and warning lights. In our homes, we use alarm clocks, calendars, and kitchen timers, as well as notes on the refrigerator. In the office, there are lists, bulletin boards, memos, and the wristwatch alarm.

In the rest of this chapter, I will describe a number of different ways to use external memory supports. The use of effective supports can not only save time, but can free you from worrying about forgetting something important.

☞ TYPES OF SUPPORT

Related Reminders

Your world is full of items that can be used as memory supports. Nearly any physical object can be used to trigger your memory at a later time. When the object is directly associated with what you want to remember, it is a *related* reminder. When it is not connected with what you want it to help you recall, it is an *unrelated* reminder. (Remember the string around your finger?) With either type of reminder, the key is to place the object in your way, so that you cannot ignore it. The object then automatically remembers for you.

To illustrate a related reminder, if you need to stop by the bank to deposit money, crumple up a dollar bill and stick it in your shirt pocket. Don't just slip it in flat, because you might forget about it. You want it to be odd enough to intrude gently on your attention at some later time.

Suppose you need to call your travel agent after lunch to set up a last-minute business trip. As you leave for lunch, put the yellow pages directory on your office floor behind the door, so that you will bump it with the door when you return. These related reminders will automatically grab your attention and memory because you can't avoid noticing them. Here are some additional examples:

- Watch on the wrong wrist (turn in time cards)
- Phone receiver upside down (call headquarters)
- Two pencils on your chair (order more office supplies)
- An empty pill bottle in your pocket (get a refill)

Unrelated Reminders

Related reminders are a wonderful way to help prompt your memory. But you are often in a situation where you can't find something related to what you want to remember. You don't have a toothbrush in your office to remind you of the dentist's appointment. In other instances, you may simply be unable to think of a physical object to represent what you need to remember. What object can remind you to set up a conference with your supervisor?

In these cases, an unrelated object will do. If you need to call a customer later in the afternoon, put a rubberband around your wrist. If you have to check with your accountant on a business expense, put a ring on a different finger. When you use an unrelated reminder, be sure to make a quick mental association between the object and the task so that you don't forget what it was supposed to remind you of (see Chapter 5, "Associate"). Be careful that you don't find yourself in a situation where you are staring at the string around your finger, unable to recall what it is supposed to remind you of! The following are some additional unrelated reminders:

- A paper clip on your shirt pocket (set up sales meeting)
- An upside-down picture on your desk (prepare monthly summary)
- Your wallet in a different pocket (call a client)
- The wastebasket on top of the file cabinet (meeting at 2:00)

Lists

When confronted with a number of minor tasks, or objects to purchase, make a list. Too often, the busy businessperson will try to juggle and edit mental lists during the course of the day. This is an unwise practice from two perspectives. First, excessive time is spent on mentally manipulating these lists, time that could be used for other purposes. Second, the lists must be continually revised as objects are located or tasks are completed.

A better system is to have a fixed location on your desk, wall, or pocket for a list pad. At the start of each day, generate a new list consisting of unfinished items from yesterday's list and new items for today. Refer to it throughout the day and update it. Copying it over repeatedly will help the effectiveness of list making as a memory support.

Writing Pad or Appointment Book

Written records can be an effective way to manage daily memory burdens. The most common support of this type is the appointment book. If you use an appointment book or calendar, its function should be clearly designated. Don't let it be a general catch-all for random notes or laundry lists.

To use an appointment book effectively, you should *always* enter every appointment. Failing to enter appointments when they seem obvious, or when it is inconvenient to get the book out, will eventually lead to confusion.

Note Card

A 3 by 5 index card is another portable written support. A separate card should be used for listing each day's worth of short-range tasks and assignments. As with the appointment notebook, the card should be carried at all times. One manager at a manufacturing company spends much of his time floating around the work area. He always has a 3 by 5 note card and a pen in his shirt pocket. Whenever he sees something that needs to be done or checked up on, he jots a quick note on the card. His employees are well acquainted with "the card" and appreciate its value to the supervisor. If they have a special request or problem, they make sure that he writes it on the card. As long as he does this, they can be sure that it will get attended to when he returns to his office.

Card Files

A card file can provide an invaluable memory backup for your most critical business information, such as meeting agendas, office policies, or client information. This card file should be small (3 by 5), clearly indexed, and in a convenient location in your office. A business card file is useful for organizing names and personal data on professional associates.

Use a separate card file for each purpose. The amount of information on each card should be minimal. The card file is efficient because it allows one to quickly discard outdated entries to minimize clutter. The card file is not meant to take the place of a file cabinet, but to provide a large amount of information in a quick-to-reference, easily updatable form. This type of support is especially appealing to a motor-oriented person because of the physical activity connected with flipping through the cards.

Other People

Often we are coerced into remembering for somebody else. A colleague requests that you send a copy of your report when you finish it in two weeks. So you try to keep this fact in mind until you are done. In this instance, the person is really asking you to do the remembering for him or her. Because this kind of request benefits another person instead of you, turn the requests around. Ask the person to remind you the day before the favor is due. If you make it clear that you are putting the burden back on the other person, you will diplomatically remove yourself from one more unnecessary memory burden.

☞ TIPS ON USING SUPPORTS

Be Systematic

The key to successful support is consistent, systematic use. If you rely on a regular support technique to reduce memory burdens, use it *all the time*. One account executive always puts a paperclip on his watchband whenever he needs to make a call to a customer, and always takes it off as he dials the phone. Therefore, whenever he sees the paperclip on his watch, he *always* knows that he needs to make a call. There is never any doubt.

If you use any support—a calendar, a notebook, a rubberband around the wrist—in an inconsistent manner, then you have the extra memory burden (and anxiety) of trying to remember whether you remembered to use it! Develop as many supports as you need, but be sure to use each one for a specific purpose, and use it consistently.

Diversify Your Supports

Beware of the "all eggs in one basket" syndrome. When one junior executive started with a marketing company, they gave her a fancy appointment book with numerous compartments and pads for all possible purposes. It was so comprehensive and handy that she found herself depending on it to record all her business and personal information, from addresses of friends to business expenses. Unfortunately, she lost it. As a result, she found herself confused and disoriented—as if part of her mind had been ripped away. She eventually recovered it, but only after she had spent considerable time tracking down all the information she had stored in it.

Some time management firms offer specialized, all-purpose organizers that can be used to get your entire life in order. It is certainly efficient to have everything centralized, but there is the risk of losing it. My advice is to diversify your external supports, and use different notebooks or calendars or appointment books, each for a different class of activity and information.

Be Selective in What You Support

If you use supports for everything—names, company regulations, and important statistics—you may run into several problems. First, you will fail to develop your abilities to attend, associate, and rehearse. Memory is like everything else—when you exercise it, it gets stronger.

Second, you have the extra memory burden of figuring out where all the necessary information is. The time spent trying to determine which information got put where can be more effort than simply committing it to memory. One indication that a certain piece of information should be memorized rather than supported is if you find yourself writing it over and over again.

EXERCISE

Describe your major supports and rate each one in terms of its effectiveness.

		How Effective?	
Support Technique	VERY	SOMEWHAT	NOT
1. _____	_____	_____	_____
2. _____	_____	_____	_____
3. _____	_____	_____	_____
4. _____	_____	_____	_____

What aspects of the useful supports make them work for you? What can you do to make your less efficient supports more effective?

Have some of your friends or colleagues developed their own special supports? What makes them work well?

MANAGING YOUR MEMORY

In the following chapters, the four-part memory management system just described is applied to a variety of memory problem areas. The training sessions I've run for business executives in memory techniques have revealed a striking array of memory-related needs in the business world. When executives are asked about memory problems, their most common reply is, "I have an awful memory for names!" In reality, the speaker's memory for names is probably just as good as it is in any other area. It's simply that when it fails, it presents a greater problem—immediate and intense embarrassment. Since remembering names seems to be the most common problem area, and the penalty for forgetting is, or seems, severe, we'll take up applying our memory system most extensively to names. But improved memory skills can measureably enhance your performance in a variety of other areas.

Personal Information: Memory for personal data will increase your effectiveness in establishing relationships and developing trust among your business associates.

Conversations: The ability to remember one-to-one discussions will save considerable time in checking what was discussed or decided, and make you a more trusted and reliable communicator.

Reading Material: The skill to handle loads of complex written information about your company, profession, the marketplace, and the competition is vital to developing your career.

Meetings: Focusing on, and remembering, what transpires during a meeting will make you a more effective and informed participant in the business activities of your organizations.

Lists: Being able to manage mental lists of ordered facts, data, or procedures can increase your work organization and enhance your ability to keep track of ongoing business processes.

Tasks to Accomplish: Improved task memory can play a direct role in increasing your work efficiency—knowing where to be at what time, and what tasks must be taken care of.

Tasks Completed: An ability to keep track of what you have finished, and what you haven't, will eliminate time wasted in rechecking and backtracking.

Numbers: Having the company statistics and production figures at your immediate recall can help in making decisions, as well as your selling products and ideas.

Making a Speech: Public speaking for small or large audiences requires a precise and dependable memory for what you want to get across.

Examinations: Keeping up with business and professional developments often requires periodic examinations, and memory management can enhance your information recall abilities.

Each chapter in this part is written as an independent unit, and most follow the same basic structure:

- An introduction, giving an overview of the particular memory difficulties in the area the chapter deals with
- The four-part memory system applied to the topic: Attend, Associate, Rehearse, and Support
- Exercises to help you make a direct and personally relevant application of the memory skills
- A Memoreview at the end, to provide a brief summary of the central points covered in the chapter

Select the topic that you need help with the most and read that chapter first. Carefully study the tips provided and apply them. You will see immediate improvement in your ability to manage memory. Experiencing your own progress will motivate you to continue enhancing your memory skills and develop them further.

8

Names

When people talk about their memory problems, their most common complaint is difficulty remembering names. Over three-quarters of the people I have surveyed stated that they could use some help. People intuitively understand the importance of name memory and have a high regard for those who remember names well. Recall the immediate sense of respect you feel for an acquaintance who remembers your name, or irritation at the person who repeatedly asks, "Now, what was your name again?"

Names are important for a number of reasons. A name is the most personal possession we have. We may change our address or switch to another company, but our name is one thing that is relatively permanent. It is one of the things we hear most in the course of our lives. And we are constantly tuned into it, so that someone saying our name across a noisy room can immediately grab our attention.

Nearly everyone has a personal story to tell about an awkward situation in which he or she could not remember the name of an important business or personal acquaintance. The pain you experience when you let someone down by forgetting his or her name is not easily forgotten. And this emotion tied up with names and introductions makes name memory even more difficult.

When you worry about forgetting someone's name, you are more likely to do just that. This concern about introductions can become a crippling cycle—you worry about forgetting names, which causes you to miss someone's name as you are being introduced, which causes you to worry even more about future introductions, and so on. This problem can become so severe that some people actively avoid certain business/social situations because they are convinced they can't remember the names of the people they will meet there. Their fears, rather than their memory, become the major obstacle to having an adequate—or better—memory.

The best advice for these people is: Relax! One way to help overcome this worry is to identify *exactly* what you are afraid will happen if you forget a name: Will you get fired? Lose a friend? Look stupid, faint, or miss a sale? Then make a rational approach to reducing that particular concern. Often, the fear is much worse than the reality.

A little success can often do a lot to put a person at ease and build confidence. A small amount of practice will help you improve your name memory markedly. And even if your name memory does not become perfect immediately, people will usually forgive an occasional lapse.

Aside from the emotional issues, names present some unique memory difficulties. First, when you were forming memory habits during childhood, remembering names was not that important. There were relatively few people in your life, and you had plenty of time to learn their names—relatives, teachers, neighbors, and classmates. You didn't need to remember the names of casual acquaintances, because your parents and teachers took care of these details.

As an adult, you *now* have a large number of acquaintances, and you must acquire the new skills to enable you to remember them all.

Another reason why names are difficult to remember is that many are abstract or unfamiliar. Names such as "Charles Trefanno" or "Valerie Greysome" do not automatically remind us of concrete objects or common experiences. In fact, you may have never seen or heard of the word "Trefanno" before in your life, so when Charles is standing in front of you, you have the dual task of remembering a new face and a completely new word.

A third problem with names is that there is potential interference: many people share the same first or the same last name. Have you ever met Sally Jones, and then Susan Jones, and gotten the two names confused? This high degree of overlap between different names results in occasional memory mixups.

A final problem with memory management of names is background confusion. Frequently when you meet people there are many distractions hampering your ability to concentrate on their names.

You may be distracted by a new environment, strange noises, or interruptions from other people. Even the very person you are meeting may distract you from his or her own name. A person's unusual voice, clothing, facial features, or mannerisms compete with your ability to capture a name.

In this section on name memory, you will learn techniques to help you overcome some of these difficulties. You will be shown how to focus on a name better, work the name into a format that is easier to remember, take advantage of opportunities to practice the name, and employ external aids to record names more effectively. But you need to promise yourself one thing before reading any further: Never tell anyone again that you have a bad memory for names. This is self-defeating. And besides, you actually have a good name memory that has just been badly managed in the past.

> "Many years ago, as part of the reporting-for-work routine," says one top executive, "I met the head of the department in which I started working as a shipping clerk. I remember the thrill I experienced when, two weeks later, he called me by name as he passed me in the cafeteria. To this day, I have a special feeling of good will toward that manager" (James McMahon, *Supervision Magazine*).

☞ ATTEND

Don't Be Self-Conscious

When we are introduced to someone, we are often thinking about how we look or what impression we are making. This inward focus competes with getting a firm grasp on a person's name. In an instant, the name is gone and we must face the embarrassment of asking for it again.

This can be avoided by preparing, just before being introduced, to focus *only* on the name. Dwelling on the impression you will make may not enhance it. Your careful consideration of a person's name, to the exclusion of all other distractions, may do more in the long run to impress them than anything else you could do at the moment.

An executive at one seminar confided to me that he constantly found himself concerned with how he looked to his new acquaintance—and missing the person's name as a result. But he insisted that this was part of his job, because it is vital for him to look sharp and make a good first impression. I suggested a simple solution. He was to locate a rest room just before he was to face a round of introductions, make any necessary adjustments to his appearance, and, secure in the knowledge that he looked all right, get that concern off his mind. If this wasn't possible, then he was to use a little positive suggestion: Repeat to himself, "I will focus on *only* the name when meeting this new person." If you have his problem—and many of us do—try my suggestion.

A special type of self-consciousness can involve a person's *own* name. If it has an unusual sound or is commonly misspelled, thinking about it may create a distraction for the owner. People who frequently experience their own name being "butchered" during introductions—who hear themselves called "Granson" rather than "Granton," or "Davis" instead of "Davies"—become alert for these mistakes and consequently may miss the other person's name while being introduced. Try to avoid this memory distraction by spelling out your name as you give it to them, or providing them with a clear image or rhyme to clarify you name (see Chapter 19, "Introducing Yourself"). But do this only before or well after you hear the other person's name, or this in itself will be a distracting influence.

EXERCISE
What distracts your attention most when you meet another person?

Your physical features: Do you have an unusual one? Do you worry about whether your hair is combed?
Sound of your voice: Do you have a speech difficulty? Are you concerned about sounding nervous or uptight?
Your clothing: Are you afraid you don't look stylish? Is your shirt tucked in?
What you are saying: Are you afraid your conversation seems stupid or unimpressive? Do you worry about what to say next?
Your own name: Is it odd-sounding or difficult to pronounce?
The person's physical features: Is he pleasant-looking or formidable?
The person's voice: Does she sound happy, or irritated with you?
The person's intentions: Will he become your friend or client?

If your greatest attention block does not jump out from this list, monitor yourself during the next few introductions.

I will not provide remedies for each problem because they will be specific to your personal situation and needs. I encourage you to generate a few solutions for yourself. Remember that half the battle is simply becoming aware of your poor habits.

Repeat the Name Out Loud

Another way of attending to a person's name is to say it out loud once it has been given to you. Saying the person's name lessens the chance that the memory of it will fade before you can get a hold on it. It provides a sensory-memory sound to hold on to for several seconds longer.

If you are introduced to a man whose name (you believe) is Paul McHenry, parrot back to him "Paul McHenry, glad to meet you." This repetition serves several different functions. The exact pronunciation of the name can be cleared up. It is easier for the new acquaintance to correct you than to correct a friend who may be doing the introducing. He may respond, "No, it's Raoul McHenry, not Paul McHenry." Some shy individuals will mumble or rush through their own name when they give it, in order to avoid seeming self-absorbed. Repeating their name back to them will overcome this problem of unintelligibility.

Repeating the name is a good habit even if the name is simple—Bob Smith, Mary Johnson. A person is always pleased from hearing his or her name spoken, even in simple repetition.

Discuss the Name

Another easy technique to help keep your attention focused on the other person's name is to ask questions about it. If it is unusual, ask the person about the national or ethnic *background* of the name. If you hear a name that is odd, ask the person to *spell* it for you. If you see the name on a name tag, this gives a comfortable entrée to saying it aloud and to talking about it.

Many names may remind you of someone you know personally, or have heard of. If you meet Wendy Disney, ask if she is related to Walt Disney. You should also ask the person if he or she goes by a *nickname* or shortened version—does Thomas go by Tom, or Jennifer like to be called Jenny?

At first, "name talk" may feel a little awkward or invasive, but most people enjoy discussing their name and appreciate the interest this reflects. A person's name is often their most prized and valuable possession, and caring about someone's name suggests that you care about them.

Allow me to raise a caution flag on this point: When a name is very unusual or possesses negative implications, be careful asking about it. For instance, I met a person called Jim Crapanzano. When he introduced himself, he sheepishly admitted that, "Yes, that really is the way you pronounce it!" In the case of very unusual names, you can gracefully skirt the direct comment by simply saying something like, "I bet you really get tired of people commenting on your name."

Learn More about the Background of Names

Increased knowledge of the historical and functional background of names can increase your attention to them. There are a number of books in the library on the derivation of modern surnames. Centuries ago in England, people were given names that told something about them, where they lived, their occupation, or some idiosyncracy.

- Where they lived: Poole, Hill, Woods, Rivers
- What they did: Taylor, Cook, Smith, Fisher, Hunter
- Their father's name: Robertson, Johnson, Paulson
- Physical trait: Armstrong, Short, Brown, Longfellow
- Behavior trait: Lovejoy, Powers, Singer

The original purpose of a name was to label an individual according to something unique about them. We do that today with nicknames like Red or Stretch or Lefty. Studying name derivations as a hobby can make paying attention to and learning them much easier.

Fix the Name in Your Mind during Small Talk

Engage in "light" conversation while you get the name fixed in your mind. Keep your short-term memory clear of any deep thoughts or complex information so that it can have sufficient room to hold on to the name.

Here is a common mistake during introductions: Soon after you have heard the person's name, you ask additional personal details: Where do you work? Where are you from? In a few moments, you have overloaded your short-term memory with extra details and the name gets bumped out. Instead of deep or task-oriented conversation, ask what the person thinks about the weather, the traffic, or a local sports team.

If you are not proficient at small talk, pick out some mundane topic of conversation (a news item) before you go to a gathering where you might meet new people. Do it beforehand, not when you are face to face with someone, because searching for a topic could consume your precious short-term memory resources and bump the name.

Study the Person: Face, Voice, and Posture

A name does not exist in isolation, but must be attached to the actual person. If the name is dangling in your memory by itself, without a clear memory of the individual, it is of less use to you.

Construct a "person memory" to attach the name to. Concentrate on the distinctive features of the individual's face (visual), the quality of his or her voice (auditory), or on posture, gestures, and movements (motor). When meeting someone, select *one* aspect of the person that you believe will be the best memory trigger.

The face may be the best part of the person to concentrate on because that is what you look at during a conversation. Take a particular, unusual feature of the face and concentrate on it. The following is just a sample of the type of face survey you could conduct in your search for the single, distinguishing facial feature:

Nose: hooked, crooked, pugged?
Hairline: receding, full?
Ears: big, droopy lobes, protruding?
Chin: pointy, cleft, rounded?
Eyebrows: bushy, narrow, plucked?
Mouth: thin lips, teeth missing?

The voice is another distinct and useful cue to hook with the person's name, especially if you are sensitive to sounds. Just as no two faces are alike, the sound of each person's speaking voice makes a distinctly different voice print.

Texture: gravelly, strained, nasal, breathy?
Intensity: soft, loud, abrasive?
Tone: high, low, melodic?
Accent: foreign, regional?

Finally, all people have a personalized way they hold and move their bodies as they interact with others. Try to key in on the following dimensions:

Head: nodding, cocked, tilted forward?
Arms: folded in a unique way, used in gesturing?
Posture: slumped, rigid, leaning?
Walk: limping, rapid?

EXERCISE

Studying individuals is a matter of habit. To become comfortable with the techniques, practice first on the characters in movies and television shows instead of someone you are meeting.

Study the faces, voices, and movements of the individuals on the screen. Follow a set procedure for the face (mouth, chin, nose), voice (tone, intensity, accent), and posture (walk, hand gestures). Deliberate practice will allow you to become adept at quickly scanning and remembering each person's unique features.

Learn Only a Few Names at Once

One of the most brutal assaults on your memory is the group introduction. When you go to a function where you don't know the guests, the host or hostess often feels obligated to introduce you to the others "en masse." It may be a social courtesy, but it does you little good! The group introduction frequently causes embarrassment because you feel as though you should remember everyone's name after the brief run-through.

When you are confronted with this situation, there are two ways to maneuver around it. Try to catch the person in charge before the group introduction, and ask if he or she could walk around the room with you and introduce each person, individually. If the crowd is too big or the host(ess) is too busy, say that you understand he or she is busy and you can take care of introducing yourself to the other people.

If these tactics fail, then bravely endure the group introduction. Catch the first two or three names and ignore the rest. Learn these few names while the others are being introduced. After the mass introduction is over, circulate on your own and reintroduce yourself to the others. Approach the others individually or in small groups of two or three. Learn these names thoroughly before going on to another group.

Go to the Function Early

Although it may make you feel a little awkward to be the first to arrive at a party or a meeting, it is an exceptionally good way to gain extra time to focus on individual's names and avoid the anxiety and confusion of group introductions that late-arriving individuals must suffer through.

As each person arrives, spend a few minutes getting to know the person and the name. As the next person enters, you can switch your *full* attention to his or her name. Another advantage of arriving early is that you can hear the name repeated a number of times. As people are introduced over again to the new people who have just arrived, you can listen in.

☞ ASSOCIATE

Focus on, or Create, Your Own Name Tag

Visual persons can often remember a name by seeing it in their mind as it was spelled out for them on a program list, place card, or name tag. Their ideal social gathering is one where name tags are worn by all participants, and the printing is bold and easy to read. Allowing the guests to make their own name tags facilitates visual associations because each one looks distinct and different.

If name tags are not part of the gathering, you can still create your own. Carry around a small tablet of paper, a pack of small cards, or a notebook. During the introduction, reach for a slip of paper and write the person's name on it. Write it slowly and deliberately, talking about it while you do. The individual will be pleased that you took the effort to record it, and you will produce a distinct visual imprint of the name.

Ask for a Business Card, First

Another way to help fix a visual image in your mind is to request a business card when you *first* meet a person rather than when you part company. This way, you can look at the name while forming an association. Take a moment to comment on the name after you have received the business card. Collecting business cards first will also ensure that you don't forget to do it later. How often do you get interrupted, and forget to ask a new acquaintance for a card?

Imagine the Name in a Printed Form

If the person's name is not available in printed form, you can use your imagination to create one. Picture the name printed on the person's forehead or chin, or generate an imaginary name tag and imagine the person wearing it. People who create mental name tags usually imagine them in a favorite location—on the forehead, on the cheek, or over the top of the head like a crown. It's best to think of a name tag somewhere about the head because it makes it more likely that the name will pop back to mind when you see the face next time.

These imaginary tags make a more distinct memory impression when they are seen as written in an unusual *style* of lettering (old English, script, or block letters) or spelled out in an odd *substance* (grape jelly; masking tape). One friend confessed that she visualizes the name written out in fire over the top of the person's head.

An administrator of a large business uses this technique to keep track of all the staff members under him. As he sees the person walk toward him, he recalls the image of the mental name tag which he created for them and can simply read the name off it.

Generate an Unusual, Exaggerated Mental Image

When you meet a person, you can convert his or her name into a visual picture in your mind. A person named Mary Perkins could be imagined in a wedding dress (marry) holding a huge coffee pot (perkins). Bill Singleton could be seen in your mind with a huge duck bill strapped to his face (bill) dancing with an enormously overweight single woman (single ton).

Distinct and exaggerated mental pictures are more likely to stick in your memory than ordinary ones. In addition, you will have more fun making them. Use wild colors, unusual sizes, and strange shapes. The image does *not* have to duplicate the name exactly, but it should be close enough to trigger it in your mind. For a woman named Fran Walters, an image of her holding a huge orange fan while a waterfall gushes over her head should be sufficient to bring the correct name back to you.

Listen to People Say Their Own Names

Sound-sensitive persons are especially attuned to subtle variations in a person's voice, and can form a distinct auditory imprint of the person saying his or her own name. When you hear a person recite his or her name, concentrate on this for a few moments. Try to duplicate it on a mental tape recorder and do a couple of quick playbacks in succession. This can provide a quick trigger for recalling the name if the person calls you on the phone, or speaks directly to you again.

Say the Name Out Loud to Yourself

Another way to form auditory associations is to say the name aloud to yourself. Repeat it several times, over and over. This is not for rehearsal, but to catch its unique *rhythm*—"Freddie Lawton, Freddie Lawton, Freddie Lawton." Make it more distinct by putting an odd emphasis on the name. Pronounce it with an emphasis on the wrong syllables—"freddIE lawTON." Try inserting a few extra syllables—"FrED-dI-e LaW-yA-tON," mocking the style of a fire-and-brimstone preacher.

Play with the sound of your own vocalization as you repeat the name. Say it in a "funny voice," imitating Count Dracula or Mickey Mouse. Give it a nasal inflection, whisper it, or try your imitation of a distinct regional accent. The goal of these techniques is to create an unforgettable auditory image for the name—a sound that is unique.

Make Up a Phrase or Rhyme with the Name

Another auditory association technique is to generate quick *phrases* to describe what the name means to you. It is similar to the visual image, except the representation is put in a statement rather than a mental picture.

For the name "Toni Sanders," say "Toni the Tiger kissed Colonel Sanders." The name "Sheri Settle" could lead to "A good sherry can set well on the tongue." Some additional illustrations include:

Sandy Weaver: It's hard to weave sand into cloth.
Glenn Snyder: The spiders live down in the glen.
Cheryl Lopez: Her share always leaves low pay.

Another, related approach to auditory name memory is to create a *rhyme*. If you are basically poetic, or if you have more time to construct one, try a sing-song phrase. "Frederick Downing is afraid of drowning!" "Jessie Baxter has a juicy backdoor." Here are a few more:

James Butler spreads jam and butter.
Lila Nichols lies about pickles.
Kevin Eagen is caving in again.

Neither the phrase nor the rhyme has to be a literary masterpiece. They are quick auditory devices to get a lasting hold on the person's name. Beware of spending too much time generating these, because this may take attention away from other information you should be processing. If you find these easy to create (after practice), use them. If not, focus on some other association strategy.

EXERCISE
How good a poet are you? For each of these names, try to generate a simple phrase and rhyme. The quicker the better. It doesn't need to be publishable—just memorable.

| Judy Pitman | Samuel Thatcher | Walter Pembroke |
| Sarah Wilburn | Ashley Goodson | Stephanie Hope |

Generate an Unusual Story with the Name

When you have some extra time to create an association, try making up a short story. Create a tale incorporating distinctive features of the individual's name. If you met someone named Phillip Granbury, you could imagine a story where you and he had to take a trip in his car to find where his *grandma* was picking *berries*, and on the way you had to *fill up* his car with gasoline several times. Meeting Marcel Brookshire, who happens to be bald, may lead to a story in which Marcel helps you build a huge house out of *marble*, with a smooth round top, which is built over a bubbling *brook* and has a distinctive church *spire* in the front.

Trace the Name with Your Hand

Are you an "air writer," someone who writes words in the air to see if they are spelled correctly? You can use this technique with names also. When introduced, trace out the name with your finger on an imaginary tablet. If you are a cautious type, conceal your hand under a table or in your pocket. If you are bolder, write in the air in front of the person you are meeting. This gives your muscles a chance to register the name in memory, and gives you a few minutes to absorb and pay closer attention to it.

A motor association can also be generated by writing the name on a piece of paper. You may not even need to look at it—the hand movements will forge the memory. Napoleon was apparently a motion-oriented person. As the story goes, to remember new names he would write them on a sheet of paper and then immediately throw it away.

EXERCISE

Try air writing the following names:

    Melanie Richards   Cathy Gregory
    Joe Harrison   Thomas Langsford

Did the writing make an impression? Give your fingers a chance to participate in name memory. Try finger writing in a few introductions to see if the technique works for you.

Tie Together the First and Last Names

Imagine the first and last names in motion, changing, or interacting with each other. The first and last names can be bumping against each other like bumper cars in the amusement park, or the first name riding on top of the last name, like a bucking bronco and rider. Or the names could be imagined crumbling into dust like dried parchment, or being inflated like two elongated balloons that a clown has tied together. For Margarette Levin, the word "Margarette" could be viewed as having a desperate death grip on the Levin. Any way you can stack, tie, glue, or superimpose the names can result in an effective, active association.

Connect the Name with Someone Familiar

Many of the new people you meet share the same first or same last name (or both) with individuals whom you already know—friends, relatives, coworkers, historical personalities, or current celebrities. Imagine the familiar person interacting in some way with the new person. In this way, the familiar name serves as a memory association link to the new name.

Peter Schultz could be imagined being introduced to a formal gathering by Secretary of State Schultz. Or Jack Stuart could be seen with the actor Jimmy Stewart sitting on his lap. Besides these famous persons, personal friends can be used to connect the new person with someone familiar to you. Imagine the persons *physically* interacting—hugging, kissing, wrestling, or shaking hands.

Make a Quick Acronym for Small Group Introductions

The following is a name association technique of limited application, to be used when introduced to a small group of persons who will maintain *fixed* locations for a short while. Assume that you walk into a conference room and are introduced by first name to five people sitting around a table in this clockwise order: Mary, Edward, Susan, Aaron, and Byron. As you are frantically repeating these names in your short-term memory, convert the first letters of their first names into an acronym—MESAB. This emergency "bridge association" will help you hold the names temporarily while you form more lasting associations.

EXERCISE

Draw on any of the techniques discussed in this section to construct an association for each name. Practice the same technique over and over, or try a different approach with each one.

Cindy Gardner	Jay Harris	Anita Mitchell
John Johnson	Brenda Lewis	Jason Bennett
Robert Kaufmann	Allen Lutrell	Gloria Ramsey
Julie Stevens	Peter Holland	Leonard Parish

If you have an unusually large number of names to remember, try creating a permanent set of associations to use anytime you encounter some **common** first names. Here are some suggestions:

Robert: He is a robber, with a black mask on.
Mark: He has a huge **x** marked on his forehead.
Mary: She has a wedding veil draped over her head.
George: He is "gorgeous."
Betty: She is gambling (betting) at a card table.
Frank: He has a hot dog in his mouth.
Susan: She is spinning on a lazy susan.
Bruce: He is covered with bruises.
Cindy: Cinderella, sitting in the cinders.
Thomas: He is playing on the tom-toms.

Make your own set of associations for these:

Barbara	Joan	Karen	Bill	Matt
Carol	Linda	Sharon	Doug	Jerry
Debbie	Sandy	Michael	Fred	John
Helen	Marie	Don	Greg	Phil
Cathy	Jennifer	Steven	David	Brian

Form name associations for everyone you encounter, even though you may never see the person again. The more you practice, the stronger a habit making name associations will become and the more easily and rapidly you will be able to form them. Use encounters with the people listed below to sharpen your memory skills:

Waiters and waitresses
Salespersons at retail stores
Football players highlighted during games
Celebrities noted in the newspaper or television news
Recording artists mentioned on the radio

☞ REHEARSE

Repeat the Name in Your Conversation

While talking with the person after an introduction, make a point of including his or her name several times in the conversation: "What do you think of the future of your company, Jane?" or "Carl, I agree that your view is one that is often overlooked." This habit forces you to remain partially focused on the person's name even when you get into substantive discussions. It also allows a check on whether you got that name correctly.

Rehearse Names When Alone

A substantial portion of your day is spent alone—commuting, dressing, walking. Rather than letting your thoughts drift off on their own, review the names of people you have recently met. When you are alone, talk to yourself and say the names out loud as if you were seeing the people again. If you cannot remember an individual's name immediately, search for it now while you have the time, or write a note to look it up after you return to the office. Better to be caught now than when you meet the person again.

Sometimes, it is necessary to "carve out" this alone time. A life insurance agent with a large company makes frequent trips to the bathroom whenever there is a social gathering with numerous introductions. His coworkers noticed this odd behavior and began kidding him about his lack of bladder control. He confessed that he needed the solitary time for rehearsing names of persons he just met. After meeting two or three people, he retires to the men's room to repeat those names and make sure they are "fixed" in his mind before coming back for more.

Review Names with Others at the Gathering

When you have learned a number of new names at a business or social gathering, reinforce these efforts by discussing the people with a friend. Scan the room with your acquaintance and practice naming each person. Ask whether your friend knows any of those people. Which ones? Discuss unusual features of the people you have just met. It helps to hear both yourself and the person you are talking with saying the new names again.

Once you are confident, go back into the crowd and try your own hand at some introductions. If two people you have met apparently do not know each other, step in and introduce them. This will aid your rehearsal for both person's names.

Take Pictures of New Acquaintances

A visual record of the new people you meet can be an invaluable technique in your rehearsals *during* and *after* the event. Instant camera photos are best because they are immediately available for on-the-spot name reviews, and they can help others learn names as they get passed around or posted on the wall.

If you don't use instant film, but have it developed, go to one of the one-hour processing labs. The extra expense will be money well spent, because the sooner you get the prints back, the less likely you will be to have forgotten the persons' names. Write the names on the back of the pictures.

Another value of photographs is as a support for your memory. A file of pictures, gone over periodically, can help shake the dust off some old memories.

Use the Name When You Say "Good-bye"

We all use standard parting phrases as social niceties: "Take care"; "See you later"; "Keep in touch." Never waste a good-bye—it provides an excellent opportunity to practice a name: "Take care, Susan." "See you later, Tom." "Keep in touch, Penny."

This forces one last rehearsal and demonstrates to the individual that you cared enough to learn his or her name. Many people can remember a name through a brief conversation, but few can say good-bye using that name an hour later. Use the name in good-byes on all occasions, even if you know the person well. It makes good-byes to old friends a little more special.

Use Business Cards to Rehearse Images

Business or personal cards provide a useful vehicle for strengthening and rehearsing name associations. Keep the cards in a convenient location at your desk. Get out your card collection and review the individuals on a regular basis (before you go home?) by flipping through them one at a time. Update your file periodically. Put your older, well-rehearsed and memorized cards in a support file, and add new cards as you acquire them. As your sort through them, spend a few seconds with each card, recalling the association you created for that name. Also recall the person's appearance, voice, and mannerisms.

A business card file close at hand can turn idle time into productive time. One executive uses his cards to fill time spent "on hold" on the telephone. He pulls out his business card container and flips through the names of people he has recently met. (If you try this, be sure to write down the name of the person you are holding for, so you don't get it confused with the names you are rehearsing.)

Review New Names at the End of the Day

Most people have certain behaviors that they go through at the end of each day: They put out the cat, set the alarm, brush their teeth. Add one more behavior to your set of day-end "rituals"—rehearse the new names that you have learned during the day.

Before bed is an ideal time because it is usually free of attention-grabbing distractions. Also, research has shown that material learned just before going to sleep tends to be better remembered, because it does not have any interfering experiences immediately afterward to disrupt it.

☞ SUPPORT

Get a List of Names ahead of Time

To avoid the memory traps involved in meeting a large group of people at once, get a list of individuals who are expected to be at a particular gathering. Spend some time studying the list before you go, so that each name will be familiar to you during the actual introductions, and you won't struggle to understand a name as it is pronounced ("Was that Prangster, or Bannister?") or be surprised by unusual (Sampson Toogood) or foreign (Frederika Jurkowska) ones. You will at least recognize each name from the list you have studied.

Recently, an acquaintance was organizing a social gathering.

When he called one friend to invite her, she asked who else was coming. He told the names of the other people he had invited, most of whom she did not know. At the party, she learned the other guests' names very quickly. When her host complimented her on her exceptional name memory abilities, she confessed that she had copied down the names as he had recited them on the phone, so that she could familiarize herself with them.

Stick with Somebody Who Knows All the People

In the Roman era, wealthy individuals used to have a special slave called a *nomenclator*. The function of this slave was to walk beside the master and whisper the names of other people they approached. In a similar manner, modern politicians use a *prompter*, or local political party officer who is well acquainted with the constituency.

You don't need a nomenclator for routinely remembering the names of people you meet. But when you go to a reception, a convention, or a meeting where you don't know many people, it is a good idea to make friends with someone who knows most of the people there. As you approach various individuals, your in-the-know acquaintance can slip you the names and a quick description ahead of time. This will make the name easier to absorb during the actual introduction.

Record Names Afterward

Immediately after a meeting, a function, or a conference, write a list of any new names on a sheet of paper or dictate them into a portable tape recorder. Store the names in a special file in case you lose some after several days. As you are compiling your list, scan your memory of the faces at the party. If you have lost some of the names, get them from the host(ess) when you call the next day to say "thank you."

If you use an audiotape support, have *one* tape reserved exclusively for the names of new acqaintances. On the tape, identify the gathering at which you met these people before you record the list of names.

Create a Backup Business Card File

As mentioned in the Rehearse section earlier, after you have invested sufficient rehearsals on a name to set it firmly in your long-term memory, route the business card to your support file. This is a "reference library," in case you need help later digging up the name of an old acquaintance. Organize the file alphabetically and/or by professional function and company.

When you first receive a business card from a new acquaintance, write the date, time, and occasion on the back. This can act as a memory safety net. Have you ever flipped through your stack of business cards and had no idea who two or three of the people were? If you have some clues on the card concerning *where* and *when* you met them, it may help you recapture who they are.

MEMOREVIEW: Names

ATTEND
Don't be self-conscious.
Repeat the name out loud.
Discuss the name.
Learn more about the background of names.
Fix the name in your mind during small talk.
Study the person: face, voice, and posture.
Learn only a few names at once.
Go to the function early.

ASSOCIATE
Focus on, or create, your own name tag.
Ask for a business card, first.
Imagine the name in a printed form.
Generate an unusual, exaggerated mental image.
Listen to people say their own name.
Say the name out loud to yourself.
Make up a phrase or rhyme with the name.
Generate an unusual story with the name.
Trace the name with your hand.
Tie together the first and last names.
Connect the name with someone familiar.
Make a quick acronym for small group introductions.

REHEARSE
Repeat the name in your conversation.
Rehearse names when alone.
Review names with others at the gathering.
Take pictures of new acquaintances.
Use the name when you say "good-bye."
Use business cards to rehearse images.
Review new names at the end of the day.

SUPPORT
Get a list of names ahead of time.
Stick with somebody who knows all the people.
Record names afterward.
Create a backup business card file.

9

Personal Information

At Fairfield Enterprises, Peter Maxwell is known for his ability to deal with people. Peter started his career as a junior-level account manager and, in the brief span of five years, managed to pass rapidly through seven positions to his present slot as vice president of operations. His was a classic story of a meteoric rise through the hierarchy.

Peter is admired and respected by all those who work under him, and he has become almost a legend within the company. People constantly look to him for advice and support, and confide in him. He always gives the impression that he genuinely cares for other people. A colleague with similar career aspirations asked Peter how he manages to garner such a high degree of loyalty among those who work with him.

His response was surprising in its simplicity. Peter said, "I have always followed two very simple rules. First, when talking with employees, I always ask them how they are doing and *really* listen to them and remember what they say. Second, when I see them the next time, I inquire about that bit of personal information that they shared with me earlier. Nothing else can establish you as a caring individual as quickly as listening to and remembering what people tell you about themselves."

Many people overlook the importance of personal information in routine dealings with business associates. Details of one's personal and business activities that are routinely shared with others—a ski trip to Vail, the $2 million account that you just landed, or your recent work on the office policy committee—are very valuable. Although someone's long discussion about his or her work with a community service organization may seem tedious or irrelevant, it can become a great help in establishing and maintaining personal relationships.

Most people are impressed with somebody who remembers personal details about them. Think of those people with whom you work who seem automatically to command respect. Most likely, they are people who take the time to remember and inquire about something you have told them.

Remembering personal information can also supplement name memory. Occasionally, you will unexpectedly run into an acquaintance at a restaurant, a conference, or the airport. Even though, because the meeting has taken you by surprise, the person's name doesn't come to you immediately, you may recall some item of personal information more quickly. The concrete fact that this person recently bought a new sailboat may come to mind faster than the more abstract name. In this circumstance, use the personal information immediately while your mind searches for the name: "Is your new baby still keeping you up all night?" or "Are those golf lessons helping your swing?" More often than not, your acquaintance will miss the fact that you haven't used a name. Then, when you do recover it, interject it in the conversation.

☞ ATTEND

Focus Your Personal Greeting

"What's happening?" "How's it going?" "What do you know?" We all use these stock phrases to bridge the gap between meeting an acquaintance and reestablishing contact, but we usually ignore the answer because we are simply interested in breaking the ice. One man I know routinely greets people with "What can I do *to* you, today?" and is amused because nobody ever notices.

This initial contact does not have to be a waste. Make a concerted effort to determine what *is* new in the other's life. Vary stock greetings so as to get a response: "What have you been doing the past week?" "You look great! What have you done with yourself?" If the person responds with a stereotyped, empty "OK, how about you?" follow up with another probing question. You would be surprised at how much data you can unearth if you make this initial greeting more directed and purposeful.

Collect One Piece of Information Each Time

Whenever you see an acquaintance, make a habit of gathering *one* piece of personal information. This provides an ice breaker for the next time you meet, and shows that you are genuinely concerned. Most people will happily share the most important current events or concerns in their lives with you. If they provide you with numerous details, catch one or two items; then, if you don't remember the rest, you'll still have something to go on.

Each time you see that individual, update this memorized information by asking about it, and add one additional piece of data. Most people have common themes running through their personal or business lives—for example, the mountain log cabin they are building, or their efforts to earn an aviator's license.

Search for Common Ground

As you gather personal data, try to find something that you have in common—a client, a hobby, or a favorite restaurant. Shared personal details are especially helpful in several ways. First, they will make it easier for you to pay attention to what the person is saying. The second benefit is that the other person may remember you better, and more fondly, if you share something in common. It will make reestablishing contact easier when you meet again. Finally, finding a common ground will create an easier foundation for forming associations by connecting the new information with your earlier experience.

Comment on Their Appearance or Mannerisms

People often display obvious clues to their occupation, life-style, and beliefs. Observe such things as class rings, charm bracelets, necklaces, or campaign buttons. When a person has a distinct accent, ask where he is from. If you notice that a person is wearing an expensive pair of running shoes, find out if she jogs.

While in someone's office, glance around for pictures on the desk or mementos on the wall. In the parking lot, check for bumper stickers or parking decals on the car. In more informal settings, insignia and names on T-shirts, sweatshirts, or baseball hats often symbolize something important to the people wearing them. Ask.

☞ ASSOCIATE

Create a Mental "Snapshot" of the Fact with the Person

Try to "see" the person and the personal information linked together in a mental picture. If your friend went on a deep-sea fishing trip to the Bahamas, create a snapshot in your mind of a giant fish sitting next to him on the sofa. When a colleague is taking night courses for a CPA degree, have her posed for an imaginary picture in a brightly colored academic robe and a ledger book under her arm.

Make your mind into a mental photography studio. The pictures can be quick and simple, but make the images as odd, exaggerated, and unusual as you can. To your mind's eye, the more distinct the mental snapshot, the more likely you are to remember the data.

When possible, condense the personal information into a *single* symbol or word. Then visualize it printed on the front of a T-shirt, or baseball cap, or as a tattoo on the person's arm. For a lawyer, "create" a shirt with a balance scale on it. Mentally image a physician wearing a baseball cap with a stethoscope on the front.

EXERCISE

Try creating simple images for the professions listed below. Use the appropriate one to facilitate forming an association **next** time you encounter such a person.

Consultant	Programmer	Office Manager
Commercial artist	Mail clerk	Banker
Journalist	Vice president	Sales representative
Accountant	Secretary	Librarian

Construct a Sentence Using the Name and Information

Another way to remember personal information is to describe it to yourself in a "catchy" phrase. Your friend Peter Samuels has been elected treasurer of a local computer club. To make this memorable, you might say to yourself, "Peter Samuels treasures his computer." Susan Travers recently took a Caribbean cruise, so make it into a quick phrase: "Susan Travers travels by cruisin'."

The best auditory associations are short, one-sentence descriptions that include the person's name and the information. If you can use rhyme, this helps. Tom Eaton was put in charge of the Western division of the company—"Tom Eaton's out West, making it the best." Often there is not enough time to search for a way to construct the sentence so that it rhymes. Then, just a play on the name is a simple way to make it stick. If Fred Forrest has bought a new fishing boat, say to yourself, "Fred is fishing *for rest* with his boat."

Imagine the Person Performing the Activity

For a motion image, pretend that the person is interacting with the event or information. Bob McGuinness began keeping bees as a hobby. Imagine him being pursued by a huge swarm of bees, being stung repeatedly and leaping high into the air in pain with each sting. Mary Horton went through the training course to become a notary public. To remember this, imagine Mary with a huge notary stamp hanging around her neck, putting her seal on everything that she passes—trees, sidewalks, and animals too slow to get out of her way.

Another way to involve activity in the association is to relate the person to someone else whom you already associate with that activity. For example, you could imagine bee-keeping Bob interacting (talking, shaking hands) with another friend who tends bees. Or think about Mary sitting in the same office as another notary public you know, chatting, hugging, or arm wrestling.

☞ REHEARSE

Comment on the Information When Taking Your Leave

When you say good-bye, comment *one* more time on the new personal information. "Take care, Alan, and let me know how your California sales conference turns out." "Good luck on the Turner contract, Pauline."

As with many of the tips in this book, this involves a simple change in habits. Rather than generic parting comments such as "See you later" and "Keep in touch," use the person's name *and* some personal information on each end of a conversation.

Recall the Information before You Contact Them Again

You occasionally run into friends and acquaintances unexpectedly, but most encounters are scheduled and can be anticipated ahead of time. Before you go to someone's office or call on the phone, take a moment to reflect back on the personal data you discussed the last time you were together, and rehearse them.

If you are not planning to contact someone, but happen to be in an area where you *might* run into him (his floor of the office building, for instance), recall the information that he has recently given you. If you do bump into each other, you are prepared; if you don't, you have slipped in an extra rehearsal.

Ask about This Information the Next Time You Meet

Be sure to comment on the personal data the next time you talk to that person. At this point, you can experience the payoff of your memory management efforts. There are other uses for a store of personal information, such as in making personnel evaluations and locating resources (a pickup truck or a housepainter). But a vital part of personal information memory management is using it to demonstrate to others that you care about them.

Personal Information

☞ SUPPORT

Keep an Information Card on Each Associate

If you are in a profession where you interact on a regular basis with a broad range of people, nurturing these contacts is important. Create a card file using a separate card for each business associate. List all the pertinent business and personal details about each, and update it on a regular basis.

Even if the personal facts seem obvious, record them. Personal details seem to slip away, especially if they appear ordinary at the time. Have you ever talked to someone and asked about her company, forgetting that she had switched companies six months ago in a heated dispute with her boss? Remembering correct information can be of great value, but pulling up outdated or incorrect data can be embarrassing.

Keep this file readily available so you can refer to the information before you call, write, or visit the person. Have his or her card in hand while talking on the phone so you can inquire about specific information and update it immediately.

Jot Personal Information on Business Cards

Use business cards to store a limited amount of personal information. Use the *back* of the cards for personal details. If you've just been handed a card, write the information on it as you talk to the new acquaintance. This slows the person down, giving you more time to process the data. It also demonstrates your concern about what they are telling you.

To jazz this support technique up a bit, consider carrying a business card folder in your briefcase. When someone provides you with new information about himself or herself, pull out the proper card and write the new information on it.

EXERCISE
Reach into your desk drawer and pull out your stack of business cards. Have you written anything on them or are they clean? If you have written

on them, what kinds of information did you record? Do you make use of this information after you have written it down?

Get an encyclopedia or a biographical dictionary. Select a famous person and memorize two pieces of information about that person that you did not already know.

Tomorrow at work, select a colleague and find out **one** piece of personal information about him or her, and memorize it. Do the same thing for a different person each day. Be sure to comment to the person about the information a day or two after you learn about it.

MEMOREVIEW: Personal Information

ATTEND
Focus your personal greeting.
Collect one piece of information each time.
Search for common ground.
Comment on their appearance and mannerisms.

ASSOCIATE
Create a mental "snapshot" of the fact with the person.
Construct a sentence using the name and information.
Imagine the person performing the activity.

REHEARSE
Comment on the new information when taking your leave.
Recall the information before you contact them again.
Ask about this information the next time you meet.

SUPPORT
Keep an information card on each associate.
Jot personal information on business cards.

10

Conversations

Much information in the business community is exchanged one-to-one, through conferences and conversations. As important as these activities are, relatively little attention has been directed to how this form of communication can effectively be committed to memory. Remembering conversations is difficult for several reasons. First, few people plan out exactly what they are going to say and how they want to say it. This means that as a listener, you have simultaneously to translate, organize, and memorize the person's message. Your efforts to figure out what is being said detract from your ability to remember it.

Another difficulty with remembering conversations is that important information is often mixed in with the trivial. Separating the two can be tedious effort. Conversations can also occur without warning—someone calls you on the phone, drops by your office, or runs into you in the hall. You don't have time to prepare yourself or clear your head of other issues that may be on your mind.

Conversations can be chopped up by interruptions or knocked out of your memory by new tasks that pop up immediately afterward. As you talk to a colleague in your office, the phone rings. When you pick up the phone, that person leaves. Then your secretary interrupts the phone conversation because an important client has arrived to discuss a new contract with you. Ten minutes into the discussion with the client, you have forgotten what the suggestion was that your colleague made in the first conversation, and the date of the appointment arranged over the phone in the second.

Finally, never underestimate the importance of conversations, especially for auditory persons. For them, one-to-one chats may be the primary means of conveying information. People whose auditory mode is weak may wrongly assume that a business conversation is simply a preliminary stage to a written document. But for a sound-sensitive person, it may *be* the document.

👉 ATTEND

Find a Stopping Point in Your Present Task

You are catching up on unfinished paperwork when a coworker drops by your desk. Although you try to listen, your mind is only half there—you are still back on your unfinished work. When your friend asks for your written comments on two points, you automatically agree and she leaves. Immediately, you return to your paperwork and five minutes later you realize that you have forgotten what your colleague asked you to do.

Many conversations fall prey to the half-here, half-there problem. It is nearly impossible to pay attention to a conversation if there is something else on your mind. An unfinished task can be an attention hog and stay on your mind until it is completed. The remedy is to reach a clear stopping point if you can't complete a task before entering into a conversation. If someone calls when you are in the middle of reading an instruction book, ask if you can call her right back. When someone pops into your office and sits down, ask him to wait for a minute while you reach a stopping point. Or better yet, see if you can come to his office after you are through. Let your callers know that you want to give them your undivided attention. It is better to risk appearing impolite by putting them "on hold" for a moment than to forget what they have said.

Look Directly at the Person

When dealing with someone face-to-face, stay visually focused on him or her; distractions in the environment can compete for your attention. The best arrangement is to have a discussion area located away from your desk. This ensures that material on your desk will not steal your attention while you are in conference. In a small office, put the visitor's chair off to one side of the desk to avoid looking across your desk while you talk to someone.

Talking on the phone requires a special effort to stay focused, because you can't look at the person you are talking to. Set the phone on a separate side table, away from other distractions. Keep a small tablet in front of the phone for taking notes, jotting down thoughts, or creating associations about what is said. Focus on this tablet in place of the individual's face.

Prevent Interruptions

A significant difficulty in managing the information in conversations is having them chopped up by interruptions from others. Have your secretary take messages for you and turn away visitors. Turn on your phone-answering device, or take the receiver off the hook. Close your door after people walk in. If the person you are about to talk to sees these actions, he is assured that you are taking him and the meeting seriously.

Although these suggestions may work for some people, many of you work in environments that demand that you be continually accessible while in your office. In this work setting, remove yourself by going to a more isolated area such as a conference room or an office that is currently empty.

If discussions are a routine part of your job, locate a little-used room to which you can retire for frank and important discussions during times when distractions are high. You will get into the habit of always listening while in this room, and the other person will appreciate your serious approach to what he or she has to say. When attending professional conventions, use this same procedure: avoid central areas and retire to out-of-the-way spots for discussions.

Ask Questions

Regardless of the nature of the conversation, get into the habit of asking questions. This has several beneficial effects on your effort to attend. It will train you to follow carefully what is being said, so as to avoid redundant or foolish questions. More important, it forces pauses in the flow of information and allows you to exercise some control over the pace.

In a conversation, the rate of the incoming information may exceed your capacity to process it in short-term memory. Questions help to slow down the pace and thus give you more time to capture and associate the information. "Now, is this the point you were making?" or "Could you state those two points again?"

If you are uncomfortable interrupting the person at odd times and are afraid you will forget your questions, keep a tablet in front of you. Write your question down, then wait for a pause to ask it. The other person will often notice you writing down your thoughts and pause so you can ask your questions.

Separate Main Points from Filler

People are not typically skilled at conveying information in a direct and organized manner in conversations. To make matters worse, most of us are unskilled at separating out primary from secondary points. In a continual stream of auditory information, it is not that easy to select out the important points.

Think of yourself as a detective hunting down clues which are hidden among extraneous material. Remember that the person talking to you is probably untrained in organizing thoughts and emphasizing key ideas.

Break the "Think Ahead" Habit

A common bad habit in conversation is thinking ahead. As the other person is speaking, you are busily planning what you are going to say in reply. But if you are thinking about what you are going to say, then you cannot effectively listen to and remember what the other person is saying. This may require that you become comfortable with pauses in conversations. Our culture does not seem to tolerate such reflective breaks in the conversation and puts a premium on fast interchanges. If these breaks in the discussion make the person you are talking with uncomfortable, try saying, "I'm just thinking about what you said."

Conversations

To correct the think-ahead difficulty, keep a note pad with you during conversations. When you have a thought or comment or criticism triggered by what is said, write it down on the paper to get it off your mind, and continue to listen. At a natural stopping point in the conversation, relay your observation. Then cross it off!

EXERCISE
Put a check beside those items which distract you during conversations.

_____ Ongoing projects in the back of your mind
_____ The next item on your agenda
_____ Phone calls
_____ Secretarial interruptions
_____ People walking into your office
_____ Items of work on your desk
_____ Happenings outside your office window or door
_____ Other

Considering your current office arrangement and work habits, how can you arrange your conversations to minimize these distractions? Are there items on your desk which you can remove? Is there some office rearrangement that you can make right now to lessen this problem? Is there a pad beside the phone to help your concentration?

☞ ASSOCIATE

Write Down Each Point

In the "Attend" section, I recommended jotting down questions that come to you during a conversation on a note pad. You should also keep a *second* note pad for recording main ideas in the conversation. (If you use the same tablet for both your questions and the person's points, you will end up with a confused record.) By separating the two on different tablets, you can see the other person's conversational flow and create an uncluttered visual association of your discussion. This second record can also be used for restating points back to your companion or for later rehearsal. The two tablets should be of different size or color so that you can easily tell them apart.

Try showing your notes to the person with whom you are talking and get his or her comments and elaborations on the points made. An additional benefit of the note pad technique is that it seems to make people stick to the point. If individuals know that you are following what they say closely, they may put more effort into organizing their thoughts.

One consultant friend accentuates this technique by carrying on his conversations at a large conference table, with a huge, flip-chart size tablet lying flat on it. On this, he translates what his conferee is saying into short phrases and symbols. It serves as a marvelous focal point for the conversation.

Imagine the Message in Visual Form

For the visual individual, it is vital to convert auditory information into a form that can be "seen." Using a note pad is one way; another is to generate distinct mental images of what is being said. If the mental pictures are not too bizarre or personalized, you may even share these images with the person you are talking to.

For instance, your friend might be discussing her concern about the sharp increase in federal regulation of the banking industry. "As I see it," you might say, "Uncle Sam is like a huge octopus wrapped around a bank, poking its tentacles in every window." Get her reaction to your interpretation—it may even help her clarify her own thoughts, or she may add to your image. Political cartoonists apply this technique very adeptly.

Restate and Elaborate on the Other Person's Comments

One of the central ideas of active listening techniques is periodically to restate the other person's own points, using his or her own language and phrases: "As I hear you, this is what you are saying...." Don't try to interpret or elaborate what you have heard;

simply give it back. This provides the associative benefit of hearing the points stated again, in your own voice. Do this particularly when an important point has been made.

After giving this verbatim restatement, embellish or elaborate on it. As a general rule, state your conferee's points first and then give your own interpretation of them. "As I see it, this means that . . ." or "From what you say, this series of events could follow. . . ."

Make the Conference Mobile

Sometimes a motor-oriented person needs to be physically active in order to stimulate memory associations. Rather than staying on one location, try talking with someone while walking down the hall, around the block, or to some other part of the building.

Being tied to the phone can also be restrictive for a motion person. To get around this, try an extra-long handset cord or speaker phone to free you up and let you pace. A car phone is also a useful motion association aid because your physical setting and experience is continually changing as you talk.

EXERCISE
If you need practice remembering conversations, get hold of some audiotapes on business topics that interest you. Although these do not directly duplicate a conversation, the idea is similar. Get a personal, portable player and listen while you jog, walk the dog, drive the car, or walk to your office. Becoming more actively involved with the information will improve your skill at remembering the substance of conversations.

☞ REHEARSE

Periodically Restate the Main Points

Several times during a conversation, list the topics covered and the conclusions up to that point. This cumulative list establishes an effective rehearsal pattern and keeps the conversation ordered and on track. In my experience, the people who most successfully deal with others are those who can keep the conversation focused by using this technique.

Review the Important Points on Parting

Never end a conversation without taking a last chance to summarize briefly what has been said. Either you or the person you are talking with should write the main ideas, decisions, and action plans on a chart, a blackboard, or a piece of paper. This helps both of you agree on the exact wording, and ensures that there are no misinterpretations or forgotten points.

☞ SUPPORT

Don't Piggyback Another Task on a Conversation

At the beginning of this chapter, I remarked that it is a bad idea to pick up another task immediately after you have finished talking to someone. Wherever you happen to be, take a minute after it is over to reflect one last time on the information you have gained. Don't pick up another activity until you are sure that the message has settled in your memory.

Create a Conversation Message File

If you spend a considerable part of your day receiving information through conferences, it may be essential to create a card file for conversations. Organize your cards by topic, day, or person, depending on the particular demands of your business activities. Write a brief summary of the major points on the card. Indicate whether the conversation was in person or on the phone.

For those of you who have a microcomputer on your desk, create a file for each person with whom you have regular conferences. At the start of the conference, call up the individual's file onto the screen and review, together, what you talked about last time. At the end of your session, update the file by adding a brief summary of what the present discussion covered.

Use a Small, Portable Tape Recorder

As technology advances, the micro audiotape recorder is playing an increasingly important role in the daily activities of the business executive. As a memory support, its primary value is in documenting an account of a conversation immediately after it is completed. After you get off the phone or following a conference in your office, spend a minute recording the highlights of the discussion.

EXERCISE

Is there a recent occasion where you forgot what someone had told you in a conversation? Why do you think this happened? In retrospect, what technique could you have used to help remember it?

Do you know anyone who is exceptionally good at remembering what you say to him? Does he seem to do anything special to remember—anything noticable when he is with you?

MEMOREVIEW: Conversations

ATTEND
Find a stopping point in your present task.
Look directly at the person.
Prevent interruptions.
Ask questions.
Separate main points from filler.
Break the "think-ahead" habit.

ASSOCIATE
Write down each point.
Imagine the message in visual form.
Restate and elaborate on the other person's comments.
Make the conference mobile.

REHEARSE
Periodically restate the main points.
Review the important points on parting.

SUPPORT
Don't piggyback another task on a conversation.
Create a conversation message file.
Use a small, portable tape recorder.

11

Reading Material

In the past few decades, there has been a remarkable increase in the amount of printed information available to the average executive. New books appear almost daily, and specialized journals for the businessperson are constantly springing up. New machines and computers require technical manuals, and continuing education has become a mainstay of business life.

Successfully digesting and remembering written material is becoming more critical for those who want to move up—or even keep their present jobs. We are entering an information age, and the management of written material will be a key ingredient to professional success.

We all know how to read for entertainment, but few of us have learned to read to get and retain information. The following pages will help correct this.

☞ ATTEND

Read during Your Peak Energy Time

Reading is often regarded as a quiescent activity, one that should fill the time just before bed. Actually, reading is a complex and mentally demanding task best carried out during your peak energy period because of the extra concentration required. Identify that part of the day when your energy level is highest, and try to schedule at least an hour as a regular reading session.

Warm Up to the Material

Jumping right into reading a report, an article, or a business manual can be like plunging into a cold mountain stream. Ease into your reading task gradually. Your eyes need to get used to focusing on the page, your body needs to get accustomed to sitting in one place, and your brain needs to ready itself for processing the incoming information.

Before opening the book or report, spend a few minutes reflecting on what you know about the subject. This prepares your mind for new information, and helps you to absorb it more readily and connect it with what you already know.

Another warm-up strategy is to read something light first. Keep a favorite magazine or novel around your office and read a *short* section to ease into your reading. Take a few minutes to get your eyes and brain lubricated, like an experienced runner limbering up before a race.

Locate an Appropriate Area

Often, the worst place for extensive reading is your own office. There are too many potential distractions to pull your attention away. Find an unoccupied conference room or employee lounge. If considerable reading is required of most employees, encourage your company to consider establishing a small library or reading room.

Commuting time on the train or bus can provide quality reading time. If your office is near a public library, escape there to read. An isolated spot in the lobby of a nearby hotel may also substitute as a reading room. If you enjoy background music while you work, avoid it during reading. Research has shown that background music hampers reading efficiency, even for individuals who normally prefer it during other work.

Here is a final recommendation for a reading location. When

you experience something in a certain room or location, going back to the same location can help trigger the memories formed earlier in that room. If a report will be discussed in a certain meeting room, then try reading the report in that same room. Or if this is not possible, imagining yourself there while you are reading can also help you recall the material when you are actually in that location.

Set Your Reading Strategy before You Start

Once you have warmed up, don't begin reading quite yet. Survey the territory. Determine how dense or difficult the material is, and how much time you will have to spend on it. Are there convenient breaking points (chapters or subdivisions), or are you going to have to create them for yourself? Unless the document is brief, don't try to read it all at one sitting. Break the material down into several chunks; connect them when you are finished. What reading strategy are you using to read this book?

If you do not already know your average reading speed (pages per hour) for business material, make an estimate over the next several times you read. Then set your goals on an hourly basis, according to this average—down a few pages for difficult material, and up a few for easy material.

If you are off your estimate and reading is taking longer than expected, revise your goals rather than increasing your reading rate. You may be taking longer because the material is denser, and increasing your rate will result in your getting less from the material.

Reward Yourself

Work is more pleasant and easier to perform if you give yourself a small treat after each section. What are your favorite activities or rewards: a soft drink, a cigarette, a piece of chocolate candy, a chat with a friend on the phone, a cup of coffee, listening to a favorite song? Don't make the treat too exotic (a movie) or indulge in it while you are actually reading (chocolate bar, cigarette). Otherwise, it may become a distraction.

Get a Dictionary and a Pencil

Assemble the tools of your task to help you establish a proper frame of mind. Before you begin reading, put a dictionary beside you and hold a pencil. The dictionary and pencil have functional as well as symbolic value. With a dictionary at hand, you are continually on the lookout for new words, and new uses for familiar words. Without the dictionary, an unfamiliar word may cause you to miss the meaning of an entire passage and lose your concentration.

The pencil not only performs its primary function but also provides an outlet for physical motion during reading. The visual mode is stimulated by the text, the auditory by self-talk, and the motion mode by the use of the pencil. A pencil also occupies your hands so they stay out of mischief (hair twirling, scalp scratching, nail biting), allowing greater concentration on the printed word.

Stop if Your Concentration Lags

Despite your most noble efforts, you will occasionally find your mind drifting away while you read. If this happens several times in a session, your brain may be trying to tell you that it is best to stop reading for a while.

Try to determine why you cannot stay focused. Are you preoccupied with something else? too warm? too tired? or upset with someone? If you can identify the source of the problem, tackle it and free your mind of it. If you can't put your finger on it, just get away from reading for the moment. Remember that reading demands a great deal of attention; if you can't bring enough to it, your reading will not be successful.

One caution. There is a danger that a misguided effort to force your attention can lead to a chronic problem of inattention. You can end up concentrating on your concentrating rather than on the material. The same is true of underlining: you are doing it uselessly if you start to underline nearly everything. It shows that you are becoming unable to tell the important points from the unimportant ones.

If your mind frequently wanders when you read, that may become a habit in itself; simply reading will make your mind wan-

Reading Material

der. A friend of mine has continually complained that reading puts him to sleep. But with a little detective work, I discovered that he did a lot of his reading just before bed, when he was tired and ready to go to sleep. Being sleepy and reading were experienced together so often that they are now strong mental partners, and one triggers the other for him.

☞ ASSOCIATE

Read the Outline and the Summary First

If a document or report has a summary at the end, read that first. Next, read the outline or table of contents at the beginning. This will put some more information on the skeleton ideas provided in the summary. Finally, quickly page through the document looking for section headings, boldface, italic, or underlined phrases, summary sentences, diagrams, and illustrations. Don't bother to memorize these items, but let them form a general context upon which to build your associations as you read.

Discover where the document or report is heading before you start so you can file the ideas in their proper place as you encounter them. Try to figure out what the following passage is all about as you read it:

> Be sure not to run out, or you could get stranded and have to walk for some. When you buy some, you may have to pay before you get it but most often you pay after you get it. Try not to spill any on the ground in the process. There are several kinds to choose from although you can't really see the difference. Be careful not to get the wrong type because it might be against the law.

If you had known ahead of time that I was referring to the purchase of gasoline for your car, then reading and remembering the passage would have been easier. This is why getting the overall picture ahead of your reading makes understanding and absorbing the text much simpler. You don't have to wonder where the writer is leading because you have looked ahead to find out.

Double-Read the Text

When the written material is important, and you have the time, read it twice. The first time read it quickly, like a novel, concentrating on picking out the main thoughts and ideas. This creates a mental framework upon which to add later associations.

The second time through, read the text more thoroughly. Instead of skipping over minor points that don't make sense, be sure to confront them directly. Don't let an idea go until you understand it, or you may forget it. Look up new words and do your underlining during the second reading. To summarize, the first reading is to get the flavor of the text and the second reading is to come to grips with it.

I would like to comment briefly on speed reading courses. An increased reading rate may be useful for "light" written material (magazines, newspapers, novels), but if your job requires reading complex documents, reading faster will not necessarily lead to reading better. Much business reading requires pauses for critical analysis and reflection, which are not part of the typical rapid reading techniques. The speed reading courses may teach concentration skills, along with reading speed. In my view, this is the main memory benefit of such courses—becoming aware of proper attention and association skills, such as those described in this chapter.

Make a Mental Imprint of the Text

For a visual person, the printed medium provides a ready-made format for storing images. If you can remember pictures and diagrams out of books and where a term or phrase appears on a page, then you may be a strong visualizer. Study the chapter outline summary or the table of contents, fixing the words into your mind as a visual snapshot.

When important terms or phrases occur in the text, visually set them in your mind as they appear on the page. If a diagram or picture is presented, set this into a mental image by constructing it piece by piece into a whole. Pretend that you are painting a picture in your mind, putting a frame around the page.

Create Memory Accents by Underlining

Underlining and marking in the margins can be beneficial to both the visual and the motion senses. The visual benefit is in seeing the results of the markings, while the motion benefit is in the act of marking. A movement-sensitive person can often remember a certain phrase, idea, or passage through the act of underlining or highlighting it.

Unfortunately, many of us were told, "Don't mark in your books!" in elementary and secondary school, because the books had to be passed on to the next class. Now, with your own materials, you don't have to heed this—but you do. It's like being reluctant about tearing off those furniture tags that say "Do Not Remove Under Penalty of Law," even though you know the law is for the suppliers and not for the consumers. If you are still loath to write in your book, use a pencil rather than a pen. This will allow you to erase later if you must.

Marking with a variety of different colors and symbols can be useful. One visualizing person worked up a multicolor, multi-underline system: a yellow see-through highlighting pen the first time through, a blue ballpoint pen the second time around, and finally a red pen for the absolutely essential points the third time through. Margin marks consist of a check for low-level importance, an asterisk for level two, and a star for the critical passages. Design your own system so you will remember it easily.

Here are some different twists on underlining that may enhance your memory:

- If you are right-handed, underline with your left hand (or vice versa). This forces you to slow down and concentrate on what you are doing.
- Try saying the underlined word, phrase, or passage out loud as you underline it. This combines motion and auditory inputs for a richer memory.
- Trace over flowcharts or diagrams with your pencil, or do a free-hand sketch on the blank pages at the end of the material.

Form Continuous Visual Image Chains of Key Points

To enhance the memory for written material, try forming mental images of the points as they are made, connecting them in a continuous image chain. Convert each idea in the text into a simple visual image. For example, compound interest could be represented by the words "interest, interest" stacked up on top of each other. Cost overruns could be converted into a car running over dollar signs, flattening and putting tire prints all across them. For additional details, illustrations, and practice, refer to the chain method presented in Chapter 13, "Lists."

Restate Points to Yourself

There is some memory value to making the written word oral. Hearing the words spoken in your own voice will make a sharp impression in the auditory mode. The rhythm of the language, plus your own personal intonation, can considerably enhance your associative grasp on the material.

If you run across an especially important passage or a short summary section, repeat it out loud. Also recite new or complex words. If you are not alone when you read, mouth the words or phrases to yourself. Just as your own vocal sounds can form an auditory memory, your mouth movements can help construct a motion aid to memory.

Create an Imaginary Discussion Partner

To apply the phantom partner technique, mentally select a friend or business associate, one with whom you are comfortable and who is a good listener. Stop every so often and fantasize explaining the material to him or her in your own words. Conduct a question-and-answer session with this person in your imagination.

Imagine a Direct Involvement

Another association technique is to project yourself into the report or activity you are reading about. Try to envision that you are directing the construction project, training the new sales representative, or presenting the annual report to the stockholders.

How would you present it? What format and supporting materials would you need? What type of individuals would you be dealing with and how would they react? Imaginary involvement pulls you into the middle of your readings and enhances association formation through vicarious participation.

☞ REHEARSE

Discuss Material with Another Interested Person

If you have a professional friend with whom you enjoy talking and who regularly reads the same material as you, establish an ongoing discussion partnership. When new material comes across your desk, set up a time for discussing it. This will impose some structure on your reading activities, and you will have an automatic and pleasant rehearsal session to look forward to. Have a discussion meeting soon after your reading in order to receive maximum benefit from the rehearsal.

If you receive a regular flow of professional information, consider establishing a discussion session on a weekly basis. Expand your rehearsal/discussion group to include others, as long as they are task-oriented more than social.

Generate Questions and Answer Them

After reading each section, form questions about it and answer them to yourself. Don't worry if the questions don't have good answers. This technique is simply designed to make you think over and rehearse the information in greater depth.

How can this improve my productivity?
Can this project really work?
What are the three major benefits (problems) of this?

Is there a way to apply this to different companies?
Is this trend permanent, or only a passing fad?
Can I think of other examples of this in my experience?
What would my clients say about this?
Could I present this to a group in a convincing manner?

The actual questions will depend, of course, on the nature of the material that you read. What is important is to reconsider what you have read with a slightly different perspective.

Write a Summary at the End of Each Section

After each section of the report, document, or extended memo, stop reading and think about what has been presented. As you generate the points in your mind, write them down. Don't go back and check until you have exhausted your mental list. Then go back and expand your list to fill in the gaps, if any.

Recopy the Outline

Generating a written outline of the material you have read is a useful way to use motion as a memory aid. Either duplicate the outline presented in the report or document, or create your own. Some efficient students copy their outlines again and again, making them "tighter" or more compact on each go around.

☞ SUPPORT

Avoid Reading Similar Documents in the Same Session

If you have regional reports from the Los Angeles, Chicago, and New York offices, read them on separate days or in separate sessions. Four copier companies are competing for your business, and each one gives a brochure on their machine. Don't skim through all the pamphlets one after the other. Read one, reflect on it for a while, then read another.

Reading similar documents back to back will increase the chances of mixing up the information. You may remember that one region had net profits of $2 million, but forget which one. Or that one copier copies upside down and backwards, but is it the same one that collates?

Add Your Personal Index

Most books and many reports have an index in the back, with page references for each key topic, idea, person, or item. These indexes vary in quality, and it is a good idea to supplement it by generating your own index.

Whenever you read some material, you will bring your unique perspective to the task. In the back of the book or report, create your own supplementary index. When an issue or topic important to *you* is addressed, which is not included in the regular index, write it down in the back of the book along with the page number. Each additional time you come across it, add the new page number. This personalized index can be a quick and valuable reference as you refer to the document later.

Build in a Postreading Pause

Allow your mind time to absorb what you have learned, in the absence of distractions. Sit back and think about what you have read for a few minutes. Avoid starting another task immediately because this may bump out the most recently experienced information from your short-term memory, or interfere with your newly formed long-term memories.

MEMOREVIEW: Reading Material

ATTEND
    Read during your peak energy time.
    Warm up to the material.
    Locate an appropriate area.
    Set your reading strategy before you start.
    Reward yourself.
    Get a dictionary and a pencil.
    Stop if your concentration lags.

ASSOCIATE
    Read the outline and the summary first.
    Double-read the text.
    Make a mental imprint of the text.
    Create memory accents by underlining.
    Form continuous image chains of key points.
    Restate points to yourself.
    Create an imaginary discussion partner.
    Imagine a direct involvement.

REHEARSE
    Discuss material with another interested person.
    Generate questions and answer them.
    Write a summary at the end of each section.
    Recopy the outline.

SUPPORT
    Avoid reading similar documents in the same session.
    Add your personal index.
    Build in a postreading pause.

12

Meetings

The primary complaint I hear about meetings is that people just can't stay tuned in, regardless of how interesting the topic or the speaker. Meetings actually provide a manageable information flow, with plenty of time to process the material from Attend to Associate to Rehearse. But this is a two-edged sword. The pace of a meeting may be too slow, causing attention to wander to other areas. Extra discipline may be required to tame your attention resources.

Another difficulty is that some people go to meetings with a bad attitude.

"Meetings always go on too long."

"I have better things to do than to attend meetings."

"We never seem to get anything accomplished in meetings."

"The meetings cover the same topics over and over again."

"Why can't somebody besides me attend this meeting?"

If you have a negative attitude, you won't get much from a meeting regardless of how productive or useful it actually is. Your opinion will be confirmed by the fact that you are unable to remember anything important that went on! Changing this attitude may be a prerequisite for memory improvement in this area.

☞ ATTEND

Organize Unresolved Business before You Go

To bring a capacity for undivided attention to a meeting, you should have come to a clear stopping point in what you were doing just before the meeting started. This does not mean you must finish completely anything you are in the middle of. Stop ten or fifteen minutes before going to the meeting and tie up loose ends. Write a short list of the things left to do on the present project. Make an effort to consider this task securely on hold for the duration of the meeting, and forget about it.

Go Early

Plan on being one of the first people at a meeting. Find a good location and review the agenda or outline. Chat with the speaker if he or she has arrived early. Remember that the brain takes a few minutes to efficiently switch gears to process information in a different way.

Avoid Bringing Material with You to Work On

The next time you attend a meeting, note how many people bring some work or distraction with them—their mail or a report they are reading. It is noble to try to take advantage of every spare minute of extra time, but bringing work to meetings is a poor idea. It provides an ever-present attention distraction, and may prevent you from getting fully into the meeting.

Leave all your office work in your office. If someone hands you a report on your way to the meeting, put it under the table or on the floor so that it is out of your sight. Don't even glance at the document before the meeting, because if it seems interesting, confusing, or controversial, it will tease your brain and pull your attention away from the meeting.

Sit Close to the Speaker

Locating a seat close to the speaker has a number of attentional benefits in any meeting or conference. It ensures that the speaker's voice will be loud enough for you, visual aids will be clearer and easier to read, and eye contact will force you to stay tuned in to the speaker's presentation. Speakers often focus on someone immediately in front of the podium.

Besides the advantage of greater visual and auditory impact, sitting close helps avoid the person who continually whispers extraneous comments during the meeting. This fragments our ability to process and remember the proceedings. The closer you sit to the speaker, the less likely this type of person will sit next to you.

Develop Techniques to Fight Drowsiness

Don't become too relaxed and comfortable in any of your meetings. Choose a straight-backed, unpadded chair. Also watch getting too warm—take off your sweater or coat if the room is overheated.

One business acquaintance has a meeting emergency kit which she keeps stashed away in her desk, which includes items such as a pack of chewing gum, a touchstone, a roll of mints, and a mentholated nasal inhaler. Prior to a meeting, she slips these into her purse and draws on them in an emergency if she finds that she is dozing off.

Create your own emergency meeting packet. Include items interesting enough to give you a little jolt, but not so complex that they will draw your attention away. A small tactile object, such as a smooth rock, may supply enough stimulation to revive you.

Another technique to regain your flagging attention is to take several deep breaths and let them out slowly. Or tense and relax your arms and legs. Change your position in the chair. Make a subtle change in some item of clothing: tighten your belt or untie your shoes. Sometimes just a little physical change is sufficient to reactivate your focus. The lack of movement in a meeting can be a special strain on a motor-oriented person.

Find a Meeting Partner

Engage in a friendly contest with a meeting partner. Make a small wager on who will remember the most from the meeting. Arrange to get together soon after the meeting and quiz each other on the discussion topics, participants, agenda items, facts and statistics, and decisions.

EXERCISE
Consider your typical meeting habits. How frequently do you:

	OFTEN	SOMETIMES	NEVER
• Take work with you	_____	_____	_____
• Get stuck beside a chatty person	_____	_____	_____
• Sit in the back of the room	_____	_____	_____
• Catch yourself drifting off	_____	_____	_____
• March in late	_____	_____	_____

From the suggestions provided in this section, what can you do to change some of these habits to allow you to improve your meeting attention?

☞ ASSOCIATE

Speakers usually tailor their presentation around their own sensory modalities, presenting information from their strength and avoiding their weaknesses. The visual person will bombard you with charts, diagrams, overhead graphics, and handouts. The auditory person will provide you with interesting stories, quotes, and puns, and encourage questions from the participants. The motor person will move around the front of the room, punctuating the points with hand gestures.

If you happen to share the presenter's same sensory strength, you will easily remember the talk. If not, you may experience some difficulty translating the speaker's message into a memorable form.

Meetings

This "Associate" section is divided into two parts. The first provides techniques you can use to help the presenter involve all the sense modalities, and the second is directed at your personal association formation techniques.

The suggestions in the first part assume that the meeting is relatively small and informal. These ideas will be more difficult to apply in a larger or rigidly structured setting.

☞ ASSOCIATE: For the Presenter

Encourage Impromptu Diagrams or Charts

Here are some signs of a nonvisual speaker: no handouts, no slides or overheads or flipcharts, and no blackboard diagrams.

When points are made that you cannot readily see in your mind, ask the presenter to write them on the board. This may be a piece of the organizational structure, the layout of new office space, or a weak point in a job flow procedure. If the presenter has difficulty, step up and help out. If you are a strong visualizer, slip a pack of pens or chalk into your pocket before the meeting so you can provide them if the speaker can't find any.

Ask Questions

Have you encountered a speaker who spoke in a monotone, told no jokes or stories, and had little interest in anything you had to say? This person probably has a weak auditory modality. Ask this kind of person to give you his or her personal attitudes, opinions, and personal stories to illustrate points. Get other members of the audience involved in impromptu discussions. The more auditory variety you can infuse into the presentation, the more memorable it will be for both you and others in the audience.

Ask for Examples or Applications

The motor person is at a special disadvantage during meetings. If the speaker is animated, uses hand gestures, and moves around the podium, this will help. But how about the speaker who stands motionless behind the podium with hands set firmly on the sides of the lecturn? Ask this person to list points on the board, draw a diagram, or illustrate how the idea works using hands and body gestures. Encourage the speaker to describe firsthand experiences or practical applications.

☞ ASSOCIATE: For You

Draw Images or Write Words for Key Points

A useful piece of meeting equipment for a visual person is a pencil and *two* legal pads—one formal and the other informal. On the formal tablet, write down each important term and concept as it is presented. This will provide your structured visual input to store away in your mind's eye.

The second tablet is for informal scribbles, questions, and diagrams. Keep your outline tablet tightly structured and formal, and the other loose and informal. The informal tablet is for transposing the content into your personal visual images. It isn't for doodling or pulling you off into a daydream.

This split-screen approach to meeting notes can also be accomplished by drawing a line down the middle of a single page, and having the left side for the formal outline and the right for comments. Or use a spiral or bound notebook. As you open it up, the sheet on the left is formal and the sheet on the right informal.

Form Mental Pictures of the Speaker's Points

Another effective way to generate associations is to mentally link the speaker's points together in your mind. Start with the first point, stick the next one to it, and so on. During a meeting, your chief accounting officer makes the following points, in succession: A new federal tax policy will increase the amount of overhead the company must include in the cost of stock brokerage service. This will result in a drop in the January net income from investments, but by midsummer the returns will be substantial. An image for this could consist of Uncle Sam (tax) pulling the hats off of two people standing beside him (overhead up). On one side is a frowning pauper in the snow (poor January yield) and on the other side is a smiling surfer on the sand (good midsummer yield).

A meeting usually allows adequate time to construct the images, so make them as distinct, interactive, and as unusual as you can. The more colorful they are, the better they will stick with you. For more suggestions, see the *chain* method in the next chapter, "Lists."

Tie the Speaker's Points to Your Experiences

Pulling the ideas from a talk into your own area of experience can make an association much easier, especially for motor persons. Try to find a real or imagined use for each idea by asking:

"How could this improve my job?"
"Will I need such a product in the next year?"
"Have I run across something similar to this before?"
"Can I apply this in ways not mentioned by the speaker?"

Regardless of how important or respected the speaker is, don't automatically absorb everything he or she says as authorative. Run their comments through the filter of your own experience. Not only will this make a strong memory imprint, but it will bring possible inaccuracies in reasoning to the surface.

REHEARSE

Stick Around after the Meeting

Even if the meeting was long and tedious, an informal chat with the speaker after the meeting can have several benefits. If the situation does not lend itself to asking questions during the talk, write them down and save them for afterward. When your questions were cleared up during the meeting, listening to the questions of others will emphasize what the important points were, giving you another rehearsal. Even if you clearly grasped each point, this informal debriefing provides an extra rehearsal before getting back to other activities.

Discuss Points with Colleagues after the Meeting

After a meeting, discuss it with others who attended. If you have selected a meeting "partner," as suggested in the "Attend" section, set aside a block of time to debrief each other. Make it as soon after the meeting as you can, and certainly not later than the end of the same day. You can also cruise through the office and gather input from a variety of different individuals. Ask them for their impressions of what the significant issues were, and the decisions arrived at.

☞ SUPPORT

Tape-Record Your Impressions after the Meeting

For most meetings, you will have some written document: a handout, your self-generated outline, or the minutes, distributed later. Supplement these records with your impromptu comments.

After the meeting, go back to your office, close the door, and spend a few minutes recording your reflections and impressions of what transpired. Have one tape reserved exclusively for postmeeting commentary. Refer to it if there is some later disagreement over what transpired, or if you need information on some details that were not in the written records.

Create a Meeting File

The recommendations, conclusions, and decisions made during a meeting often become distorted, reversed, confused, or lost over time. Two processes occur in meetings that make decisions difficult to remember. The first is interference. In a typical meeting, many of the topics are closely interrelated, and can therefore get easily confused in your mind. Let's say that there are three proposals to reduce cost: waste reduction, time management, and future incentives. An hour of the meeting is spent bouncing these around, and by the end, your mind has merged many aspects of these plans together. All the ideas sound similar to each other.

The second aspect of meetings is that our memory tends to be selective. Even immediately after it is over, if you ask five different people about what decision was made on a controversial topic, you may get five different opinions. People selectively remember those things with which they *agree* or which they support, and forget things they don't agree with. Often, when an important idea is debated, it becomes difficult to separate the final decision from the multitude of preliminary plans. And if you aren't careful, you will most likely remember those parts that you had some input on, or agreed with.

Therefore, the meeting minutes and decisions should be closely documented by a neutral person. If no formal channel exists, write your own version of what transpired. Before you file it, circulate your version so others can indicate their agreement, or disagreement, with it.

MEMOREVIEW: Meetings

ATTEND
Organize unresolved business before you go.
Go early.
Avoid bringing material with you to work on.
Sit close to the speaker.
Develop techniques to fight drowsiness.
Find a meeting partner.

ASSOCIATE: For the Presenter
Encourage impromptu diagrams or charts.
Ask questions.
Ask for examples or applications.

ASSOCIATE: For You
Draw images or write words for key points.
Form mental pictures of the speaker's points.
Tie the speaker's points to your experiences.

REHEARSE
Stick around after the meeting.
Discuss points with colleagues after the meeting.

SUPPORT
Tape-record your impressions after the meeting.
Create a meeting file.

13

Lists

As I promised earlier, this book is not written for the budding memory expert, but for the busy person who needs some simple and quickly applicable techniques for increased memory efficiency. Most people do not constantly need to memorize long lists of items or concepts. But for those of you who need help in this area, this chapter will provide some standard but effective techniques to enhance this skill.

This ability is more important for persons who have to make speeches on a regular basis, keep an extensive product line at their immediate recall, or know all the steps in a production sequence on the spot. List memorization is also helpful when you do not have something to write with at the moment, or you are in a situation where it is inappropriate to make a list. When you think of a list of items while taking a shower, attending a dinner party, or driving your car to work, it may be inconvenient to write the points down.

The most central issue for list learning is forming the associations, and therefore, only association techniques will be discussed in this chapter. There are no special attend, rehearse, or support procedures.

There are actually two different types of lists: where information about an item's numerical *position* is important, and where it is not. If you create a grocery list, it is not important to know which is the fifth item and which is the twelfth one. On the other hand, if you are memorizing the steps in a production process, it is important to know that a requisition is Step 3 while the marketing director is notified at Step 8. The first two list techniques, *chain* and *location*, do not allow for numerical position. The third type, *pegword*, does.

☞ ASSOCIATE

Chain

With the first list association technique, the different items in the list are hooked together like links in a chain. An image for each item or object is tied together with the next one, and so on. In this manner, each item serves as a cue for the next one. Once you form the links, you can go forward from one item to the next using these adjacent links, or even backward in the series.

Assume that you have the following six items on a list: drop off some old shoes at the resale shop, mail a letter, buy paint, pick up a suit at the dry cleaners, get the car inspected, and get milk at the grocery store. You could form a chain list of these items in the following manner: Visualize a huge shoe-shaped mailbox filled to overflowing with letters, with some of the letters ripped and torn from being jammed down the top. Next imagine a large letter falling into a container of red paint, and getting so blotched up that you can't even read the address any longer.

Now see yourself throwing that can of paint at your suit hanging in the closet, causing streaks of paint to drizzle down the front of your favorite suit. Then visualize your car dressed up in a suit, with the pants on the back wheels and the jacket on the front. The next image involves your car hitting a cow who has wandered into the middle of the road. You hit its udder, splashing milk all over the road.

Be sure to turn each pairing of items into a distinct image. If you spend a moment making each link bold, intense, colorful, and out of the ordinary, the images should flow effortlessly from one link to the next in the chain of associations.

EXERCISE

Practice your chaining abilities on this list of ten objects. Make each pairing distinct and bizarre.

1. frog
2. matches
3. rifle
4. socks
5. light bulb
6. ice cream cone

7. garden hose   9. hammer
8. bed   10. bar of soap

Location

The second technique for memorizing lists involves a series of familiar locations with which you are well acquainted: parts of your home, office, or body. The general practice is to use a different location for each item to be remembered, and form a quick mental picture linking the item to the location. To recall the list later, you go through these locations in you mind and each one should trigger your memory of the object placed there.

Let's take your *home* as the first example. Get an image of your home in your mind, picturing each room. An item on your list is associated with each room. Circulate through the rooms in your home in a consistent manner so that you can easily remember this mental walk later. Try using a clockwise direction around your home.

To illustrate the technique, I will use the same items from the chain section: shoes, letter, paint, suit, car, and milk.

Dining room—shoes: Imagine muddy footprints all over the floor and furniture of the dining room.

Kitchen—letter: Dozens of mail bags are stacked in the middle of the kitchen floor. A mail truck has just dumped its contents here by mistake.

Garage—paint: Old cans of different-colored paint are spilled all over the garage floor. The colors have run together to form a paisley pattern on the floor.

Living room—suit: Several guests in bizarre pink and green checked suits are dancing in the middle of the living room. The music is turned up and the guests are having a wild time.

Den—car: In the den, you are surprised to find an old pink Edsel made into a coffee table. Its top has been sliced off and replaced by a large sheet of plexiglass.

Bedroom—milk: The guest bedroom was unfortunately flooded

by sixty gallons of milk when a milk drum was accidentally knocked over.

EXERCISE

What rooms or places in your home would you use? Pick ten to list below. Use the laundry room, closets, garage, basement, and attic if you need to. If you live in an apartment, you may need to pick several locations **within** a room to find ten. For example, in the living room you could pick the wet bar, the fireplace, and the bay window as separate locations.

1. _____   6. _____
2. _____   7. _____
3. _____   8. _____
4. _____   9. _____
5. _____   10. _____

Using a home or an apartment is the most common way to form a locations system, but you may use your office instead. In the office, use the objects you scan from left to right, as you sit at your desk: door, file cabinet, window, typing stand, computer, bookshelf, picture, coatrack, desk, and chair.

How about large lists, up to a hundred items long? Select a large house with at least ten rooms. Then select ten features within each room.

A final kind of location system can be constructed using your *body*. The advantage of the body location system is that you are very familiar with it, it is always with you, and doesn't change as your home or office could. The disadvantage is that it is more difficult to image objects interacting with your body, compared to the larger spaces of a dwelling.

Work up your body using each of ten parts to form different associations: feet, knees, thighs, hips, stomach, chest, hands, arms, neck, and head. Recovering the associated objects is then as simple as mentally tracing a path back up your body, stopping at each body part.

Pegword

At the heart of the pegword system is a standard set of number-word pairs. These particular pairs are thoroughly memorized so that they automatically trigger each other. The items in the list to be memorized are then associated with the *words* of the pegword pairs. Associating the object with the word simultaneously links it with the number.

I will present two different types of pegword systems, one auditory and the other visual. In the auditory system, each number has a word that rhymes with it. For the visual system, the words resemble the associated number visually. With each system, the goal is the same: to use a particular word as an indirect link between the number and the object you want to recall.

One caution before using the pegword system. This is more difficult to memorize and apply than the simple techniques because it requires that you memorize the standard pegword framework before you memorize any particular list of items using it. Its effective application depends on considerable practice and regular applications, and is not recommended for those who have only an occasional ordered list to master.

Auditory Pegword

The rhyme-based pegword is the most popular system.

one—bun	six—sticks
two—shoe	seven—heaven
three—tree	eight—gate
four—door	nine—wine
five—hive	ten—hen

Assume that you are on the food committee for the annual company picnic. Your task involves getting the following items: lemonade, hot dogs, beer, coffee, catsup, large trash bags, paper napkins, sugar, relish, and potato chips.

One—bun—lemonade: A large hamburger bun has a number of lemon slices jammed in between the two halves.

Two—shoe—hot dogs: An old black high-top army shoe has hot dogs sticking out of the top. There are several other hot dogs on the floor.

Three—tree—beer: A beer tree has hundreds of beer cans hanging on it, and people jumping up trying to grasp the fruit of the beer tree.

Four—door—coffee: A cup of coffee has been thrown against a closed door. Coffee is dripping down the door and bits of the cup are lying on the floor.

Five—hive—catsup: An eccentric beekeeper insists on pouring catsup all over her beehives. The bees are upset and swarming around her head.

Six—sticks—trash bags: A boy is stuffing piles of sticks from his front yard into large trash bags. The sticks are splitting the sides of the bags and spilling back out.

Seven—heaven—napkins: Several angels are taking huge stacks of white napkins and wadding them up to form additional clouds.

Eight—gate—sugar: An old rusty gate is buried in a huge pile of sugar. A woman is holding a large sugar bowl and spooning more sugar over it.

Nine—wine—relish: A wine bottle is filled with a green relish mixture and someone is pouring the runny, lumpy mixture over a hot dog.

Ten—hen—potato chips: A farmer is tossing out potato chips to feed his chickens, and they are crushing and gobbling them as fast as they fall.

As you create each mental connection, make it distinct, dramatic, glib, bizarre, or unusual. The rhyme words provided above are a commonly used set, but feel free to substitute your own.

EXERCISE
How did the location method work for your? Write down the ten items given earlier in this chapter.

Lists

1. _____ 6. _____
2. _____ 7. _____
3. _____ 8. _____
4. _____ 9. _____
5. _____ 10. _____

If you didn't do well with my locations, try your own. Go through the objects again using your personal locations and see how well the associations work.

Visual Pegword

For each of the numbers one through ten, a visual association can be used rather than an auditory one. In this system, the associated word names an object which *looks* like the numeral:

one—cane	six—plow
two—swan	seven—razor
three—pitchfork	eight—hourglass
four—mailbox	nine—lollipop
five—bicycle	ten—bull's-eye

A straight walking cane resembles the numeral 1. A swimming swan looks like a 2, with its long neck curving gracefully in a loop. The 3 is a 3-pronged pitchfork on its side. A country mailbox on a post resembles the numeral 4. An old-time bicycle, with a large front wheel and a small rear wheel forms a 5. The 6 is an old horse-drawn plow, with the thick blade in the front and a long handle behind it. A disposable plastic razor resembles the numeral 7. The hourglass is a natural image for 8. The numeral 9 looks like a lollipop. And an archery target with an arrow through the center, a bull's-eye shot, represents the numeral 10. The arrow is the 1 and the target is the 0.

Now let's apply this to another list of ten items. You ask your fellow workers what supplies they need, and keep the list in your head: pencils, desk lamp, coatrack, envelopes, new coffee pot, filing cabinet, desk-top fan, ink pad, roll of stamps, and a box of floppy disks.

> *One—cane—pencils:* A walking cane is made of a huge yellow pencil with the eraser bent to form a handle. It leaves a trail of dots on the ground as you walk.

Two—swan—lamp: A swan has been stuffed and made into a lamp for your desk. Its mouth is fixed open with a bright 100-watt light shining out of it.

Three—pitchfork—coatrack: A pitchfork has been formed into a coatrack for your office. The prongs have ripped holes in several coats hanging on it.

Four—mailbox—coffee: A coffee pot has been jammed into the mailbox. You serve yourself a cup by pulling open the mailbox door and coffee spills out into your cup.

Five—bicycle—file cabinet: A circus strongman is riding the bicycle in the center ring, trying to balance a filing cabinet on his handlebars.

Six—plow—ink pad: A huge ink pad is about an acre in size. A farmer is running a plow through it, getting all covered with ink in the process.

Seven—razor—envelopes: A giant, worn-out envelope is being ripped to shreds as a razor is scraped back and forth across it. Shreds of paper are flying everywhere.

Eight—hourglass—fan: Somebody tied an hourglass to the blades of a fan. As it is turned on, the fan's spinning blades break the glass and spew sand all over.

Nine—lollipop—stamps: A secretary is trying to moisten stamps by licking a lollipop and then wiping the stamp roll on the wet lollipop.

Ten—bull's-eye—floppy disks: A stack of floppy disks have been mounted on a target. An archer misses the center and sends the arrow piercing the entire stack of disks, ruining them.

Summary

The Chain Method

- Involves no preparation.
- Can be applied quickly.
- Does not provide numerical information.
- Is not easy to use for going backward in the list, or starting in the middle.

Lists

The Location Method

- Involves more effort than the chain technique.
- Makes the association stronger because it is personal.
- Does not provide information about the number corresponding to each position.
- Is more useful than the chain method for going backward through your list, since you can walk backward through your house.

The Pegword Mnemonic

- Is the most effective and versatile technique.
- Should be used only by *serious* list makers.
- Involves more effort to learn than the other two.
- Provides precise information about the ordered position of each item.

EXERCISE

A. Compare the effectiveness of the two pegword systems. Recall the ten items from each of the pegword lists.

Picnic Goodies

1. _____
2. _____
3. _____
4. _____
5. _____
6. _____
7. _____
8. _____
9. _____
10. _____

Office Supplies

1. _____
2. _____
3. _____
4. _____
5. _____
6. _____
7. _____
8. _____
9. _____
10. _____

Which system was easier, or were they both about the same? If you would like to, create your own pegword system in the spaces below. Maybe a combination of the auditory and visual systems would work best for you.

1. _____   6. _____

2. _____   7. _____

3. _____   8. _____

4. _____   9. _____

5. _____   10. _____

B. Sharpen up any memory technique using the following list of words:

1. clock
2. orange
3. pliers
4. automobile
5. candy cane
6. socks
7. rubber band
8. giraffe
9. football
10. scissors

14

Tasks to Accomplish

Often, it isn't the large issues or tasks that cause you problems. It's the little daily details that "slip through the cracks," causing stress and annoyance. A large part of managing these details is simply remembering what to do and when to do it. It may not be enough to depend on an efficient secretary or a detailed appointment book. In a rapidly changing and demanding environment, you need some concrete methods for keeping on top of those small tasks which pop up randomly and slip by too easily.

This chapter is directed primarily at the person whose job is *not* routine. Someone who has essentially the same kind of tasks to carry out every day will not gain as much from it as the person whose work environment is more uncertain, rapidly changing, and sensitive to the demands of several different constituencies.

Sometimes the businessperson's most difficult task is to balance a number of different tasks, miniprojects, emergencies, and appointments for a limited time. This information does *not* need to be stored in a permanent form. It simply needs to be managed efficiently until it is successfully completed.

☞ ATTEND

Prepare, in Advance, for Your Memory Load

Even in the most hectic, demanding, and fast-changing business settings, there are usually regular patterns of activity. Although you may not be able to predict when and what tasks and assignments may be thrown at you, there are usually daily, weekly, and monthly fluctuations. Take a minute to consider your own work. What part of the day, or what day of the week, is most hectic?

Anticipate peak demands and try to "budget" your attention accordingly. Keep your attentional energy free to focus on the details that crop up unexpectedly during that part of your day. Set aside small, less-important detailed tasks that can easily be interrupted for these times. You'll be more able to switch your attention quickly to the details that cross your desk.

Tackle Unexpected Tasks Immediately

When tasks pop up in the course of a business day, address them immediately, or they are likely to get dropped. Complete a task on the spot, or at least get it started by making a quick phone call, contacting a coworker for help, or having a "to do" list close at hand to note down those things that come unexpectedly. Dealing with the task immediately, even if it is only superficially, can help avoid losing it altogether. If you fail to do it on the spot, or at least start the wheels in motion through a note or call, the unrelenting flood of business activities will probably wash it out of short-term memory and away for good.

☞ ASSOCIATE

There are basically two kinds of associational techniques for tasks to accomplish. For a task that pops up suddenly and needs to be done within a few hours, you'll want to use only *minimal* effort for associating it. Remembering it for a short period of time doesn't require the formation of a permanent memory. The first three techniques below pertain to this kind of task. In contrast, there are tasks that will need to be carried out several days from now. For these situations, a more involved type of mental calendar may be required.

Image the Task with an Environmental Cue

To remember a task, think of some common object that you will be likely to encounter just *prior* to doing it. Create a mental image of some aspect of the task interacting with the object.

Suppose you will need to talk to Gerry about the planning meeting agenda before you go to lunch. On the way to lunch, you have to use the elevator. Form a mental image of Gerry caught between the elevator doors, struggling and yelling for help. Later in the day, when you do go to lunch and actually see the elevator doors in front of you, the image of Gerry will jump out at you.

Or suppose you have to call the Los Angeles office before you leave in the evening to find out whether they received an important overnight letter from you. Make a mental picture of the letter wrapped around the doorknob of your office, so that you will "see" it as you lock up your office to go home in the evening. Pretend the letter is crinkled and taped around the knob so that you will "see" it when you lock up your office.

Be sure to connect your image with an object that you are *certain* to run into, look at, or touch before the task needs to be carried out: office door, doorknob, a building, a telephone, mailbox, garage door, car, overcoat, keys, briefcase, umbrella, or coffee mug. Or have the object of the association be a person whom you are sure to encounter—your secretary, the receptionist, the parking garage attendant, or the front-desk security person. Imagine the object somehow prominently attached to that person. When you pass them later, you will be reminded of the task you have ahead by the association you previously made.

Describe the Task Out Loud

The most effective way to form a simple auditory association is to describe *aloud* what you need to do. When you need to send a sympathy card to a client, simply say out loud, "Send a card to Frank by tomorrow." Or to remember the 3:30 meeting, say, "Be sure to go to the afternoon meeting."

One hitch to this quick association is if other people are around, you may feel you look a little crazy, talking to yourself that way. There are two ways around this difficulty. When you happen to be with other people that you know, tell one of them what you need to do. "Did you know that Frank's father died? I need to pick up a card for him on the way home." Or "Are you going to the meeting this afternoon? I hope something productive comes of it."

Suppose, on the other hand, that you are surrounded by strangers. Take out your pocket tape recorder and talk into it. (You don't have to actually turn it on; just hold it up and talk at it.)

Pantomime the Motions

Another type of association for upcoming tasks is pantomiming the particular activity before you need to carry it out. If you have a letter to mail on the way home, get the letter out of your pocket and go through the motions of pulling open the mailbox slot, dropping the letter in, and closing it. It doesn't have to be an award-winning dramatic portrayal—just enough to put the memory reminder into your muscles. When you pass the mailbox on your way out, the activity should come back to you.

You can get more abstract in your quick motion images. Jennifer has asked you for a list of the members of the company softball team. Take a couple of pretend swings of a bat while you make a mental note to get this done. The director of marketing calls from Denver and asks you to feed the fish in his office while he is away on a business trip. Make a pretend swimming motion with your arms and pantomime tapping a box of fish food over an aquarium.

Like the auditory association, the pantomime may be embarrassing to carry out if there are people around. Try a smaller, scaled-down version of the motion.

EXERCISE
Select three tasks that you have to accomplish today or tomorrow:

1. _____

2. _____

3. _____

Tasks to Accomplish

For the first: select an object you will encounter just before taking care of the task and form a dramatic image with it. For the second: Try saying it out loud a few times. For the third: Go through a pantomime of the activity.

Compare the effectiveness of these three types of quick association by testing them out over several days, on a variety of tasks.

Create Mental Images for Days

For individuals who must keep an entire week's worth of activities and events in mind, the days of the week can be converted into simple images and used just like the pegword system described in Chapter 13, "Lists." Here is a suggested set of associations, but feel free to create your own:

Sunday—sun
Monday—moon, money
Tuesday—twos, toes
Wednesday—wedding, water, wet
Thursday—furs
Friday—frying pan
Saturday—chair, sat

Suppose that for the coming week, you have a lunch with your banker on Thursday, a departmental meeting on Wednesday, a memo to be distributed on Monday, and an interview with a new vice president on Friday. For the Thursday lunch, imagine your banker wrapped in a huge raccoon coat with a fur hat. The Wednesday departmental meeting can be imagined as a wedding, with all the department in tuxedos and formal dresses and with the speaker in a wedding dress. The Monday memo is in the night sky wrapped around the moon. For the Friday interview, the new officer is seen tied up and sizzling in a huge iron frying pan.

Translate Days and Times into Number Pegwords

Another use of image to recall tasks is a number pegword system to represent both days and times of the day. The hours of the normal working day can be directly converted into numbers. The days of the week can be associated with the pegword system in the following manner:

Sunday: 1—bun
Monday: 2—shoe
Tuesday: 3—tree
Wednesday: 4—door
Thursday: 5—hive
Friday: 6—sticks
Saturday: 7—heaven

For the banker luncheon on Thursday, imagine your banker sitting at a restaurant and eagerly cutting into the chef's surprise—deep-fried beehive. The Monday memo can be imagined crumpled up and stuffed into a shoe. For the department meeting on Wednesday, you decide to replace the conference table with a huge, intricately carved, wooden door. Finally, the interview on Friday can be remembered by imagining the vice president carrying a huge bundle of sticks as a present for you, and dumping them all over your desk.

Make a Mental Picture of Your Calendar or Clock

If you have a limited number of appointments, conferences, and errands per day, a mental calendar image can provide a useful memory bulletin board. I have a monthly calendar on the wall of my office. Whenever a task comes up, I write it on the appropriate day, making a point to do it with different color pens or slanting in various ways. Each entry is visually distinct. As I record the information, it automatically gets imprinted into my memory by the motion and visual action. When somebody asks me if I am free for lunch Wednesday, or if we can schedule a meeting for Tuesday afternoon, I simply call up the calendar image in my mind and check it for entries.

The face of a traditional clock can also be used for displaying mental images. On a large clock face, tack mental pictures of the tasks (objects, people's faces, etc.) in the appropriate wedge of the clock. Be sure that your mental clock face resembles that of the clock face on your wristwatch or office wall; looking at it will help to trigger these clock-face images back from memory.

☞ REHEARSE

Use Routine Daily Times to Review Tasks

A number of people manage their business detail memory more efficiently by setting aside a regular time each day to think about important upcoming tasks. One businesswoman uses three brief times: a few minutes at ten o'clock in the morning, after the initial morning rush; after lunch, to prepare for the afternoon; and an hour before she leaves the office, to get ready for the next day. These times for reflecting on the tasks ahead only have to be a minute or two long. Depending on your personal workload and how many unexpected task demands you usually get, you may need fewer or more task-check breaks.

EXERCISE
How about your typical workday? When are things most likely to slip through the cracks—in the early morning, around midday, or in the late afternoon? Plan your rehearsal times **prior** to that part of the day when you experience the most difficulty.

Pause for a Mental Check at Transition Points

During the typical workday, you change physical locations several times. For most individuals, these transition points are:

- Leaving home for work in the morning
- Leaving the office for lunch
- Leaving the office for home at the end of the day

Just before each of these changes, pause for a few seconds to determine whether you have overlooked something. Is there some task that you should have taken care of? Something you need to take with you? Somebody you promised to check with?

This is not the same as the task checks during the workday. It is a more superficial check to remind you to put that book in your briefcase, confirm the appointment for tomorrow morning, or unplug the coffeepot. Scan your work categories briefly (tasks, objects, people) to tie up loose ends.

☞ SUPPORT

Related Reminders

As you may recall from Chapter 7, "Support," related reminders are objects that have a direct and natural association with the task they are used to remind you of.

An easy related reminder for *time* is your watch. Suppose that you are stopped in the hall by someone who says that there is an emergency meeting of your department at 1:30 this afternoon. Immediately switch your watch to the other arm, or turn it upside down on the same arm. Because you look at your watch often during the day, it is sure to remind you of the meeting the next time you see it. It is important that the reminder be odd enough to trigger the memory but not so unusual that it becomes a continual distraction. Don't put your wristwatch around your ankle!

An effective related reminder for *money* matters is a dollar bill stuck in an unusual place. You receive a notice in the mail of a new high-interest IRA that has become available. If you want to drop by the bank at lunch and switch some funds to it, take a dollar bill from your wallet, crumple it up in a ball, and stuff it in your pocket. Feeling it in your pocket will help remind you of the task.

Unrelated Reminders

It is best to use a related reminder if possible. But there are numerous situations where there are no related objects available or paper and pencil to write it down, and you have to make do with what you have: standing on the bus riding to work, in a conference in another office, or sitting in a movie theater. These are situations

Tasks to Accomplish   145

where you must make do with whatever object happens to be on you or in your immediate surroundings.

A string around a finger or a knot in a handkerchief are common examples of unrelated reminders. The advantage of an unrelated reminder is that almost any object can be used to remind you of something else. The disadvantage is that you must spend a minute making the connection between the reminder object and the task—"This string on my finger means I have to fill out the personnel reports."

There are three classes of unrelated reminders: visual, physical, and auditory. Any of them should be potent enough to trigger your memory, but not so bothersome that they distract you.

A useful place for *visual* reminders is on your hands or arms because these parts of your body are constantly in your view and will get noticed. Keep a supply of wrist-sized rubber bands in your desk. When a colleague drops by your office to request a copy of your departmental report, take a rubber band out of the drawer and put it on your wrist. Make a quick mental association between the object and the task. Use different colors and thicknesses of rubber bands so that you can use more than one at a time.

An important customer calls to request more detailed information on a new product you are in charge of. If you cannot take care of this on the spot, put a paper clip on the end of your shirt sleeve, and form a quick mental link while you do it. Safety pins can also be used on cuffs or shirt sleeves.

To generate *physical* reminders, alter something that you are wearing. Most of your clothing and jewelry has a distinct feel which you become accustomed to: your watch, rings, necklace, belt, and shoes. If you change the feel, this can act as a reminder. For instance, you could:

Tighten (or loosen) your watchband one notch.
Tighten (or loosen) your belt one notch.
Move your watch to the other arm.
Switch a ring to a different finger.
Untie (or tighten) one shoe.
Move your wallet to a different pocket.
Loosen your tie.

When a colleague requests a copy of a report, you can tighten your watch one notch and make a quick mental connection between it and the request. Or during the meeting, you can reach under the table and untie one of your shoes, or slip it off.

The use of *auditory* reminders is more limited. These objects include wristwatch and calculator alarms, cooking timers, clock alarms, beepers, and computers. The obvious advantage of auditory devices is that they can be set for a precise time. The disadvantage is that there is no variety to cue you to a *specific* task: every time the alarm goes off, it makes exactly the same sound.

The most versatile auditory support device is the wristwatch alarm. Unfortunately, it can be disruptive or embarrassing when it goes off in the middle of a meeting or conference. An alternative is a small, credit-card-sized pocket calculator with an alarm function. Carry it in your coat pocket, purse, or briefcase to muffle the alarm sound.

When at home, use a cooking timer or alarm clock to trigger your task memory. If you carry a beeper, have a secretary, associate, or answering service call you at a specific time. The beeper going off will remind you to take care of the task.

There is one more place where unrelated reminders can come to your rescue. During the quiet time just before falling asleep, you often remember tasks that must be taken care of. But you usually don't feel like getting out of a comfortable bed to make a note of them, or even reaching for pencil and paper on the night table. It's likely to make you wakeful and you'll find it hard to get to sleep.

When this happens, making a small change in your immediate surroundings will serve as a reminder in the morning: Tip your lampshade, throw the book or magazine into the middle of the bedroom floor, scatter a few cigarettes on the bedside table.

EXERCISE

The events listed below might confront a businessperson in the course of a day. Using only the items which you have with you at the moment (besides your book), generate related and unrelated cues for each item.

Tasks to Accomplish   **147**

9:00 A.M.—Your secretary reminds you that you have a dentist appointment this afternoon on your way home from work at 5:30.

Related _____ Unrelated _____

10:45 A.M.—A coworker tells you that copies of the year-end report are available in the mail room. You need to pick one up before lunch.

Related _____ Unrelated _____

1:22 P.M.—You receive a memo that a candidate for the accounting position is interviewing today, and your time with her has been set for 3:15.

Related _____ Unrelated _____

3:05 P.M.—Your department is considering a new microcomputer system, and a sales representative will demonstrate the equipment at 4:30.

Related _____ Unrelated _____

People Reminders

Special Favors

Willing as most of us are to help others, we often forget about a promised favor. To avoid this predicament, have the friend who requests the favor do the remembering for you. If an acquaintance wants a ride to work the Monday after next, ask him or her to remind you the day before.

Putting the memory burden on others avoids their becoming upset with you if you forget something, and it relieves you of some unnecessary memory management chores. Make it very clear to them that they are responsible for reminding you.

One college professor was constantly fielding special requests from students: Can I take the quiz a day early? Can I have an extra day to work on the paper? Can I see you next Thursday at 2:15 to discuss my project? These requests would often come during the confusion right after class, and he would forget the request. Now, after he approves a special request, he tells the student to let him know *one* day ahead of time. He never gets blamed for forgetting special favors anymore.

Memory Partner

If a colleague of yours shares the same departmental activities and interests as you, form an agreement to remind each other just before a meeting or conference is starting, before a deadline has arrived, or when a task needs to be undertaken.

Such a relationship does not guarantee that every task and deadline will be automatically remembered, because *both* of you may forget. But it does provide a backup system. If necessary, try several different memory partners for extra memory protection.

Gab Partner

Have you had this happen to you? You ask a friend to remind you of something. Your friend forgets to do it, but *you* remember. Just mentioning it was enough to set it in your *own* memory.

To make use of this, take on a gab partner. Choose someone who doesn't mind your popping in at odd times for a quick chat. A telephone gab partner will also work. It may not be someone in your office or company, but someone who is close enough personally not to mind being called on impulse.

Office Subordinates

If you have workers directly under you, use them to remind you. Give them small tasks at first, ones that are not critical. Once they demonstrate their dependability, trust them to help you remember more important tasks. By giving subordinates this memory responsibility, you can make them feel a more integral part of the office workings. It also gives you a good way to learn whose memory you can trust for bigger decisions and responsibilities.

Service Personnel

There are many individuals who provide routine services to the busy professional, and who can also be used as memory supports. Many doctors and dentists now call or drop a postcard to remind you of your regular checkups. Ask your accountant, banker, and investment broker to remind you of regular appointments, due dates, and changes in legal regulations.

EXERCISE
How do you currently use people to support your memory? Have you tried trusting others' memories to support yours, or do you prefer to be on your own?

Do any professionals call to remind you of appointments or due dates? What other professionals could you ask to remind you when their repeated services are required?

Checklist Reminders

A portable support system is essential for a busy person. In the past, information flowed at a much slower rate. But the present fast-changing business climate almost demands a way to keep up *on the spot.*

Tape Recorder

Many executives now carry a portable tape recorder with them, wherever they go. It provides an on-the-spot task support system and the extra memory advantage of a rehearsal. A portable recorder also helps you make associations by letting you hear yourself.

Phone-Answering Machine

Your own automatic phone recorder can provide a handy list support system. If you have one on your home phone, call home each time a nonbusiness task occurs to you during the day. When you get home, your list of things-to-do is recorded for you on the machine. If you are out of the office frequently, you can also use this same technique with your office phone. Put a message recorder on your office phone and call whenever things to do pop into your mind.

Note Card

A simple card placed in your pocket every morning provides an excellent portable listing device: on it you can accumulate the tasks that you have to take care of, and track what has been carried out. At the end of each day, you have a review of what has been accomplished during the day. Any unfinished business is transferred to the next day's card.

Permanent List

For all those little tasks that need to be taken care of before you leave home, construct a permanent list to post under the light switch at the door you'll go out by, where it will catch your eye: lights off, stove off, alarm set, thermostat down (up), windows closed. Under the office light switch, your reminder list might be: books for home, calls to make, letters to mail, phone-answering machine on, files locked. A quick glance over the checklist can provide peace of mind later.

Note Pad

A large legal tablet on your desk top is a useful support fixture. Put it in a special place where it is impossible to overlook. Add new tasks as they occur and cross off old ones as they are completed. Revise this list every few hours by copying it over, and list the tasks in *decreasing* order of priority.

When you make notes to yourself, abbreviations are fine. But be careful not to make them *too* brief. All of us occasionally make a note which says "Thursday at 3:30" and we don't know what it refers to, or "Call Mr. J" and we don't remember whether it is Mr. Johnson, Jones, or Janeski. When in doubt, use the following guideline for abbreviations: If you dropped dead tonight, could your successor make sense out of the note to tidy up your unfinished business?

Sticky Notes

A variation on the note pad system has recently emerged, thanks to the all-surface sticky (Post-It) notes that have been developed. Instead of a list of items on one sheet, each item is written on a different tab of paper and stuck wherever you need it: on the doorknob, coffeepot, computer monitor, typewriter, coatstand, telephone, or chair. Rather than crossing off items as you do them, you simply throw away the little piece of paper or stick it somewhere else.

You don't even have to write anything on the piece of paper. Simply putting a small, blank piece on the phone receiver can remind you of a call you need to make, and one on the doorknob can remind you to lock the door when you leave.

Magnetic Letters

When my children were little, I bought a set of brightly colored plastic letters with magnets on the back to use in teaching them words. After my children outgrew them, I turned them into a memory support by constructing messages on metal surfaces at home and office.

Magnetic letters can add motion to the checklist technique. With a box of these letters in your office, you can turn the side of your file cabinet (or any metal surface) into a support surface. When you have a call-back to make, or a supply item to get, or a meeting at 3:00, spell it out with your letters.

This can also open up unique communication routes within your department. As others in your office discover your letter board, they may also participate by slipping into your office and spelling out messages or reminders on your file cabinet.

Monitor Board

If your occupation forces you to keep track of a number of different projects or tasks at once, a large wall board may help support your memory by showing you, at a glance, how each work project is progressing. A magnetic board, a cork board with pins, or a board with card pockets can be used.

If there are twelve different activities in your routine work, and each day requires you to check on some but not others, make a twelve-pocket wall board labeling each pocket with the name of one activity. Stick a green card in those pockets that require attention "today." As you take care of them, remove the card. As a demand arises with another project, put a green card in that pocket. These tracking support mechanisms provide a stimulating way for visual or motor-oriented persons to remember the day's activities easily.

Calendars and Appointment Books

In order to round out the support systems for tasks to do, there are the standard date books and wall calendars. Since most of you use these already, I will include only a few selected comments and suggestions. At the beginning of the year, when you purchase it, fill in all the anniversaries, birthdays, medical checkups, license renewal dates, and special occasions that you want to remember. Hang a calendar where you will see it immediately when you enter your office. If you also use a date book, be sure to enter all important things to do both in the appointment book and on the calendar.

MEMOREVIEW: Tasks to Accomplish

ATTEND
  Prepare, in advance, for your memory load.
  Tackle unexpected tasks immediately.

ASSOCIATE
  Image the task with an environmental cue.
  Describe the task out loud.
  Pantomime the motions.
  Create mental images for days.
  Translate days and times into number pegwords.
  Make a metal picture of your calendar or clock.

REHEARSE
  Use routine daily times to review tasks.
  Pause for a mental check at transition points.

SUPPORT
  Related reminders.
  Unrelated reminders.
  People reminders.
  Checklist reminders.

15

Tasks Completed

We all forget little routine details of our lives and whether we have carried out certain tasks. For most of us, the consequences of these memory lapses are not traumatic because they usually involve only ourselves. When you forget where you left your keys or whether you set the alarm, only you have to know.

Despite this, poor memory for completed tasks can have a drastic impact on your performance when the uncertainty preys on your mind. "Did I, or didn't I turn on the telephone-answering machine?" You have to go back and check, or call somebody to check for you, or simply try to force it out of your mind. This consumes your time and mental energy. Ironically, it is those things that we do *regularly* that we are most likely to forget. Things that are done constantly, in basically the same way, lose their ability to grab our attention as we carry them out.

This is an important chapter for "absent-minded" persons who frequently forget if they did something or where they put something. It is similar in some respects to the preceding chapter, "Tasks to Accomplish," but it covers more automatic, or more routine types of behavior, and helps you make what you are doing right *now* recallable an hour from now.

☞ **ATTEND**

Slow Down

Many bad habits are the result of doing things too quickly. Overweight persons generally eat faster than people of normal weight, and pay less attention to their food. The same is true of chain smoking or drinking too much coffee. These become automatic habits that sidestep our conscious awareness. Something as simple as slowing down your activity level may yield an immediate improvement in memory management.

Your psychological state tends to parallel your physical pace, or the pace of activity around you. Have you noticed yourself becoming "hyped up" and nervous around a fast-talking salesman? With rapid activity around you, your thoughts also speed up to match them. It is more difficult to process information because so much is being packed into short-term memory that little gets through to long-term memory. Slow down your rate of speech, the speed at which you walk, and how rapidly you drive. As the slowness habit grows stronger, your thoughts, attention, and memory will grow increasingly sharper.

Give a Quick Thought to Everything You Do

Many of the routine tasks that we carry out do not require our full attention—pouring a cup of coffee, taking a shower. This becomes a problem only when inattention spreads beyond the simple tasks to more complex behaviors. A simple remedy is to keep at least part of your attentional energy focused at all times on *each activity* you are engaged in, no matter how routine. Unless you make it a habit to be continually aware of all your activities, you will slip back into ignoring more and more of them.

Some people protest that they are too busy to do this. They believe that they must keep their minds focused on their overall businesses or they will fall behind. An examination of airplane accidents indicate that a significant percentage are caused by mental lapses on the part of the pilot—not paying close attention to their immediate behaviors. The same holds true of other types of vehicle accidents. The ramifications of your inattention may not be as drastic, but you can significantly improve your task memory management by always focusing part of your awareness on whatever you are doing at the moment.

Do One Task at a Time

If you have eleven tasks to accomplish by the end of the day, there are two ways to approach them: simultaneously and successively. People often choose the simultaneous approach because it gives them the feeling that they are being more efficient or productive. In our culture, there is the stereotype of the wheeler-dealer executive with three people in the office and two others on the phone, successfully delegating tasks and responsibilities to all of them simultaneously. There may be some people who can pull this off, but most people work best when doing tasks sequentially. You may be able to handle a couple of tasks at once, but sharing your attentional resources among four or five can be hazardous to your memory.

When an unexpected intrusion occurs—the ring of your phone, a call on your beeper, or an unexpected visitor—protect what you are doing. Write a quick note on a tablet in front of you. If something is in your hand, don't set it down during the interruption. Take a few seconds to deal with your present activity so that after the interruption you won't have forgotten what you were doing.

Use Nonactive Time for Pondering

Ruminating on the past or drifting into the future may be pleasant, but it should be done only when you're not engaged in some other activity. Remember that short-term memory is a limited resource, and must be used to monitor simultaneously what is going on around us, what we are thinking, and what we must do. Trying to think about one thing while performing another is doing a disservice to both activities. Each one takes away from the efficiency of the other. So to get the most out of your head, set aside a time when you are not doing something else for your think–plan–reflect time.

☞ ASSOCIATE

The associations for tasks completed are relatively simple. The useful time span for memory of most completed tasks is usually only a few hours. Therefore, the suggestions in this section will be aimed at quick, less permanent associations.

Look at It Differently

One reason you cannot find where you put your glasses or pen may be that you weren't watching when you set them down. To make observing yourself more interesting and memorable, look at what you are doing from a slightly different perspective. When you set down your keys, spread them apart on the table. When mailing a letter, stand to one side of the mailbox so that it makes a slightly different visual impression as you drop the letter in the slot. When locking a door, bend down to look at it more closely or look at it out of the corner of one eye. Squint or blur your vision slightly, or cross your eyes momentarily.

Anything you can do to see some routine action slightly differently will make a distinct and quick association. But don't do it the *same* odd way each time. Otherwise, the extraordinary will become ordinary and lose its memory impact.

Form a Dramatic Image as You Do It

As you carry out a task, create a quick mental picture of the act. Pretend you are a film editor who is adding some cheap special effects to an ordinarily dull movie.

If you are setting an alarm, imagine it exploding as you touch it. Or see it made out of gooey putty, with your fingers stuck momentarily in the mess. When you lock the door, imagine the knob flashing brightly like a strobe light. For mailing a letter, picture the large metal deposit box as a hungry blue monster opening its drooling mouth to swallow your delicious letter.

Take just a second or two to make your image, and be sure to make it different each time. Your friends will wonder when you chuckle to yourself as you lock your door on the way out of the office!

Say What You Are Doing Out Loud

While going through your daily routines, comment on what you are doing. As you file away the Richmond Associates contract, simply say, "That takes care of Richmond." If a colleague happens to be with you and you put your airline ticket in your suitcoat pocket, simply say, "I'll put the ticket in my coat pocket so I won't forget it." Make it conversational and routine, whether you are with someone or by yourself.

As you lock your door, say, "I'm locking my door as I leave the office." When setting down your keys on the coffee table, comment that "my keys are now on the coffee table next to the ashtray." Try slightly different inflections or different tones of voices each time.

Make an Odd Noise with the Object

Many objects have a distinct sound to them—doors, mailboxes, coin machines, and alarms. When you take an action that uses an object that makes a noise, enhance its sound. Flick the clicker on the ballpoint pen several times before you put it in your purse or pocket. As you set your keys on your desk, jingle them a couple of times. The switch on your phone recorder probably has a distinctive click. Listen closely for it, and flick it two or three times back and forth as you turn it on.

If you find the object–noise association useful, you can even generate a sound of your own for noiseless objects. Make a "ching, ching" sound like a cash register when you set your checkbook down someplace. When hanging your umbrella on a coatrack at a restaurant, make a quick thunderclap under your breath, or say "fwump," like the sound of an umbrella being opened.

Do It in an Odd Manner

Most routine tasks are performed the same way time after time. That is what makes them routine, as well as forgettable. You always hold the phone, buckle your seatbelt, and open a can of soda exactly the same way each time. A distinct motion association can be created by doing it slightly differently every time.

When turning off the stove, move the knob with your hand twisted at an odd angle. Or do it with your opposite hand (your left if you are right-handed). Rather than locking the door in the normal way, hold the keys between your little finger and your ring finger. A bit less efficient, but you won't forget having done it.

Perform It Faster or Slower Than Usual

Pacing is another way to establish a unique motion memory. Either speed up or slow down your normal pace. Before you leave, turn out the lights very slowly. Approach the wall in slow motion and gently ease the switch down.

When locking your door, pretend that you must do it without waking anybody up. Turn the key slowly and take it out as if you were a burglar. Set your keys on the dresser slowly, making sure you can hear each key hit the top.

EXERCISE

If you leave your car at an airport parking lot, you may occasionally forget where it is parked when you get back. Even if the lot has each section numbered, finding your car within a particular section may be difficult.

Taking the association principles just discussed, here are a few suggestions to overcome this difficulty. As you leave your car, walk to the point where you will catch a shuttle bus (in large airports) or to the terminal door (in small airports). Stop at that point, turn around and look back toward the car. Fix in your mind what the visual scene looks like, with lamp pole and buildings, while staring at the point where your car is located. Describe aloud where it is: "about forty yards to the left in line with the airport control tower," or "just beyond the second no-parking sign beyond the gate to the right." Finally, you could simply extend your arm and point in the direction of the car.

Apply the same principles when you park to go to lunch, or go shopping at a mall.

☞ REHEARSE

Use Routine Time(s) Each Day to Review Tasks

In the preceding chapter, on organizing your memory for tasks to accomplish, I suggested that you carve out a special time during the day to rehearse those things that need to be done during the rest of the day. You can use the same time to reflect on what you have already done. The two best times are in the middle and at the end of the day. Make your reflections brief.

People report an additional benefit to these "reflect back" sessions. Recreating the earlier part of the day in your mind will occasionally jog the memory of additional tasks that you may have forgotten to do. It is like throwing a fishing hook in muddy waters and coming up with an unexpected catch.

> Many executives and professional people use the weekend for brushing up their memories of the week's significant happenings. . . . The weekend solitude and slowed tempo provide almost ideal conditions for refreshing memories (Donald and Elanor Laird, *Techniques for Efficient Remembering*).

Keep a Task Diary

An extended version of the above suggestion is keeping a diary. In the traditional sense, a diary is a personal log of the experiences, moods, ideas, and thoughts during the day. The diary I am suggesting is more task-oriented. Keep a small notebook at your bedside, and before retiring, jot down the task-related events of the day and their status—completed, just started, get a bid, etc.

Although this method may take more time than the mental run-through, there are several advantages. It makes the rehearsal more memorable because visual and kinetic dimensions are included. It also creates a memory support as a by-product. Finally, it extends the reflection period. Those of you who have kept a standard type of diary appreciate that writing about your experiences can trigger additional memories. As you reflect about one task or event, this can pull another one to mind, like links in a chain.

EXERCISE
Go back over your day's activities. Can you run through everything you have done, or are there a few gaps? With some practice, you will be able to recall and review your completed tasks very quickly.

☞ SUPPORT

Use the Check-Off System

When you complete a task, assignment, or activity, make a quick physical notation of some sort. For a task written in an appointment book or list on your desk, check it off or cross through it when it is done. Form a habit that every task is not completely finished until it has been scratched off your list.

Other types of regular tasks may not lend themselves to a standard type of check-off system. For example, it is difficult to track pills that have to be taken *several* times a day in this way. Try forming an abbreviated system: Each time you take a pill, put an asterisk (*) in that day's space on your calendar, or put a "P" on it. By counting the marks, you can tell at a glance at the end of the day whether you've adhered to your schedule.

There are also multicelled pill containers that can be carried in a pocket or purse. These keep track of your pills for you, since you can tell if you've taken a pill simply by checking to see whether the appropriate cell is empty.

Always Put Objects in the Same Place

A place for everything, and everything in its place. This memory rule should apply to your office, your home, and your person. In your office, establish a specific place for everything you own and use.

If you have the occasion, observe a blind person going about his or her daily activities. The blind are—by necessity rather than choice—experts at this kind of memory support.

Do you have any "nomad" objects—items that never have a permanent place? These are probably the ones that you are most likely to misplace. As you go through your daily routines for the next day or two, identify and collect these nomads and establish a special home for each one. Turn an unused mug or pencil holder into a residence for your glasses. Use an old ashtray for your keys; the top left drawer in the desk for the checkbook.

Treat the contents of your own pockets or purse with the same consistency. Always put the same objects in the same locations and you will never have to fumble for your comb or the garage parking stub.

Be Careful about Hiding Valuables

A householder about to go on an extended trip wants to hide some valuable possession (jewelry, a coin set) or cash from a possible burglar. After hunting around the house, the owner discovers the perfect place. But on returning home, the person goes to uncover the valuables and realizes that he or she has forgotten where it is!

When you locate a hiding place, you obviously try to find one where nobody would think to look. Unfortunately, you may do too good a job and fool yourself as well.

If you have valuables that you need to protect, put them in a safe deposit box. It is a small effort and expense for the substantial peace of mind that it brings. But if you insist on hiding items at home, select *two* places right now, and use them consistently and exclusively. Selecting an impromptu hiding place just before leaving on a vacation is an invitation to a memory lapse, because so much else is on your mind to interfere with your remembering that great hiding place you found.

Keep a Lending List

When something you have generously loaned to a friend or coworker doesn't get returned, it can be a real hindrance, especially if it involves the tools of your trade.

To protect yourself, create a lending list. When you lend an item, enter the information on your list while the borrower is standing beside you holding it. Enter the date you lend it out as well as the "anticipated" return date to focus the borrower's attention on a commitment to return it. Not only will this support *your* memory, but you hope it will also create an association in the memory of the borrower about returning the item.

Hang the list on a clipboard and ask the borrower to cross the item off the list when the loan is returned. The more you can do to involve the person in the process, the more likely it is that he or she will remember to return what was borrowed.

Some people avoid keeping a lending list because they feel it gives the impression that they don't trust others. If you experience this discomfort, turn the focus on yourself by telling the borrower, "I really don't trust my own memory." If you oversee a number of people, and borrowing is a common activity, make it an office policy for each person to keep a lending list. This will eliminate any stigma about such a list.

Create a borrowing list for yourself if you are guilty of occasionally forgetting to return items. Each time you borrow something, record the date and the person you get it from. This will create a handy record for yourself, a way to form a quick association, and an insurance policy against damaged social relationships!

Mark Your Name and Date on All New Possessions

A friend of mine has a special, all-surface marker that he uses for all his possessions. Whenever he acquires something, he marks his name and the date on it. At first, I thought this was just a curious habit, but I later discovered it to be a remarkably useful technique for supporting both his own and others' memories. Whenever you lend something, your name on the object provides a visual reminder to the borrower that the item is, in fact, borrowed.

The date provides another useful function. How often have you wondered whether an item is still under warranty, or if it needs to be replaced? Along with satisfying your personal curiosity about when you acquired the object, knowing how old it is often tells you when to replace it. Many items such as glue, paint, and tape, deteriorate in quality over time, and should periodically be replaced.

MEMOREVIEW: Tasks Completed

ATTEND
Slow down.
Give a quick thought to everything you do.
Do one task at a time.
Use nonactive times for pondering.

ASSOCIATE
Look at it differently.
Form a dramatic image as you do it.
Say what you are doing out loud.
Make an odd noise with the object.
Do it in an odd manner.
Perform it faster or slower than usual.

REHEARSE
Use routine time(s) each day to review tasks.
Keep a task diary.

SUPPORT
Use the check-off system.
Always put objects in the same place.
Be careful about hiding valuables.
Keep a lending list.
Mark your name and date on all new possessions.

16

Numbers

Applying memory improvement to the area of numbers and statistics presents a unique challenge: numerical information is different from verbal information. Both letters and numbers represent simple symbols that are combined into larger units to convey information. When letters are combined to form a word, this becomes a *single* piece of information. Combining seven separate letters to form "N−U−M−B−E−R−S" yields only one item to remember. The combination of letters actually reduces your memory load.

Now compare this with numbers. Combine eight separate numbers to form the number string 7−8−2−0−2−1−5−4 and you have 78,202,154. For most people, this is still eight pieces of information. This makes the memory burden much greater.

Another general difficulty with numbers, besides complexity, is that many people have an emotional reaction to them. Having taught statistics for many years, I have noticed a broad range of negative emotions expressed toward numbers. Some view numbers as cold and impersonal. Others are suspicious of them; they feel that numbers are somehow "flexible" tools for manipulative individuals to obscure real facts. Others are simply afraid of them. They have never been comfortable with numbers and experience an automatic fear reaction when confronted with a large, statistically oriented report.

All these emotional reactions to numbers interfere with your ability to remember them. The information cannot even get into short-term memory if an emotional block closes the door.

Most other memory books present a specialized procedure for

Numbers

remembering numbers, based on a prememorized set of number-letter associations. The numbers are translated into letters, and then the letters are formed into words. This makes remembering numbers easier because through a double translation process, a six-digit number becomes a single word. I include this specialized technique in a separate section at the end of this chapter. It is *not* worth the effort and practice needed to memorize the procedure *unless* you deal with numbers a great deal and they are very important to your job.

In this chapter, there are some techniques for simplifying and digesting number information, as well as for generating a more positive and playful attitude toward numbers. I offer a wide range of suggestions for reducing the difficulty of remembering numbers by translating them into a more personal form. How do you remember your 24-hour teller code number, or the combination of your safe, or your office phone number? Chances are, you have not simply memorized a string of digits, but have personalized the numbers in some manner. The heart of number memory is developing more effective Attend and Associate techniques. (There are no Rehearse and Support sections in this chapter).

> Benton Love, of Texas Commerce Bancshares: "The executive who tells me he can't remember numbers tells me that he can't remember the significant part of his business and is operating on quicksand" (Roy Rowan, *Fortune*).

☞ ATTEND

Develop a Positive Attitude about Numbers

The gate to improved number memory will never swing open until you can confront and eliminate any negative attitudes you have. Avoiding numbers, or trivializing their value, will not do. You need to embrace numbers as an essential and important part of your business activities. Here are some simple suggestions for those who need a minor attitude readjustment.

Use a gradual approach to warm up to numbers. Start learning *one* statistic per day about your colleagues, your company, or your profession. Search different professional newsletters and magazines for the information, or read your company's annual report.

If you need encouragement, locate another person who has number "phobia" and go through desensitization together. Each of you can find a statistic a day to memorize and exchange with each other. As you become comfortable with numbers, up your quota to two or three statistics each day. Discuss them with others. The more you utilize numbers, the more comfortable you will be with them and the more naturally you will include them in routine business interactions.

Determine Which Numbers Are Most Important

Here is a perfect recipe for number shock. You are presented with a page summarizing the annual fiscal report. Top management has kindly spared you the 57-page document, but you still have 3 columns across the top—credit, debit, and net—with 36 company subdivisions down the side. One glance is enough to force anybody into a memory seizure. How can you possibly absorb all those numbers, make sense of or remember them?

Be selective. As someone is talking to you, you don't take in every word and try to remember it. You sort out his or her main points. For some reason, people have a much more difficult time doing this with a set of statistics.

Attack a set of numbers with a red pen or a yellow highlighter to make the important numbers stand out. Ask yourself, "What do I need to know a week or month from now?"

Go for Approximations, Not Exact Values

How many people are in your company? How far do you live from work? What is your annual income? In response to these questions, you might answer: "About two hundred and fifty," "six-and-a-half miles," and "thirty-five thousand." None of these answers is technically correct, but a rough approximation will do most of the time.

The obligation to be precise with statistics is overwhelming. When you are given a statistic such as "the Spokane Branch processed 4,572 documents yesterday," it looks so compelling and accurate. You feel that you are fudging if you don't remember and pass along this number precisely down to the last digit. Actually, people are not usually that interested in such precision. All your associates really want to know is that "forty-five hundred documents passed through Spokane yesterday."

☞ ASSOCIATE

Combine Numbers into Pairs or Groups

All the associational efforts described in this section are aimed at reducing your memory load by simplifying the information contained in a number set. The most basic form of reduction is to use pairs rather than single digits. We do this naturally with *dates*. The year 1958 is referred to as "nineteen fifty-eight" and not "one nine five eight" or "one thousand, nine hundred and fifty-eight."

The phone company makes use of this technique by creating two groupings from the seven numbers (three and four), rather than stringing out seven digits in a homogeneous row. And we can remember them more easily because of this. Social security numbers have this benefit, too, being separated into three groups of digits (three— two–four). Try chopping up numbers you are given into your own personal subgroupings.

Construct a Mental Chart

The visually oriented person will sometimes see numbers as a line drawing or chart. The number 9531 will be seen as a giant ski slope going from left to right. There is a large initial drop (9 to 5), followed by a more gradual slope-off (5 to 3 to 1). The phone number 275–7865 is viewed as a sharply rising mountain peak on the left, with a more gradual hump to the right.

Since this type of visual association is easier to show than

692-3420   363-6491

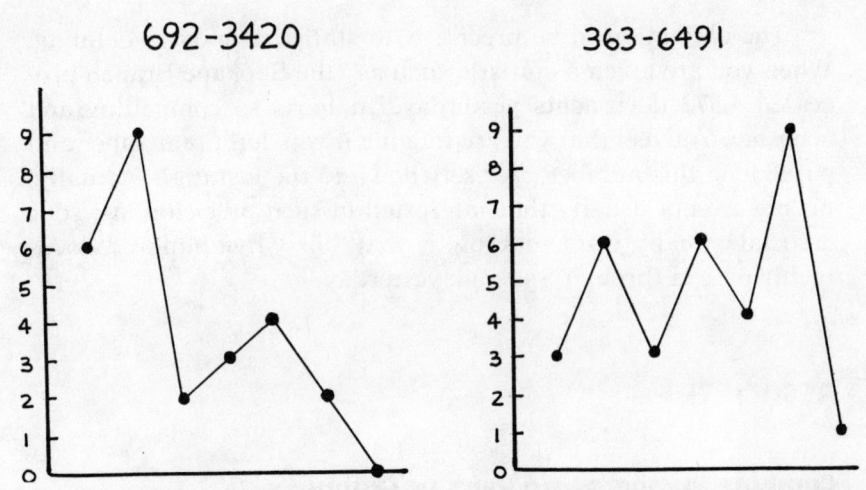

An example of the mental graph association method for remembering phone numbers

describe, see the graph above which illustrates two different telephone numbers. People who work extensively with graphs and charts (like myself) may resonate with this format and find it to be a very useful associational supplement. Others may think it is crazy. This is only one of the offerings in the cafeteria line of number associations. If it doesn't suit your appetite, move along.

Use a Letter or Word for Number Magnitude

One common technique for simplifying numbers is substituting a verbal or letter representation for the magnitude, or size, of the numbers. For a thousand, there is a "grand" or the letter K. Instead of saying that the person spent two thousand dollars on the business trip, you might say he spent two grand or two K on it.

Perhaps the simplest way to approach this association is to use the initial letter for your association: H = hundred, T = thousand, M = million, and B = billion. If you deal a lot with numbers, you might fill in additional symbols for ten thousand (TT) and hundred thousand (HT).

Also consider Roman numerals: I = 1, V = 5, X = 10, L = 50, C = 100, D = 500, M = 1000. By using this letter translation, you can also make up words to represent the numbers. For instance, the number 44 is XLIV, which could be translated into "extra liver." The primary limitation of this Roman system is that there will be a lot of X's to contend with, and there are a limited number of words containing this letter.

Make Up Phrases or Rhymes for the Number

Advertisers have used this technique with great proficiency. They understand that numbers are difficult to get the consumer's mind to remember, so they use songs, jingles, and rhymes on the radio and television. If you are like most people, you have had a telephone number jingle stick in your head. Even if the song is silly or guttural, it can be hard to get out of your memory.

With a little practice, you can apply this technique for your own use. Say the number aloud, and then create a phrase that follows the same meter and that rhymes with the number. A classic example is, "In fourteen hundred ninety-two, Columbus sailed the ocean blue." Say that you have the price $12.85 to remember. Construct a rhyme like, "Twelve eighty-five can make you come alive." Or the phone number 712–3008 could translate into "Seven twelve thirty oh eight, can sure make me feel real great."

Establish a Distinct Auditory Rhythm

Numbers often have a *natural* rhythm of their own. Saying them over and over several times can implant a catchy or unique rhythm into your memory. James Polk used the campaign slogan "Fifty-four forty or fight" to refer to the latitude of a disputed territory that he was willing to go to war over. The slogan caught on because of its rhythm and alliteration.

You may already use this technique as part of your association for common numbers. Take your telephone number or address or social security number. When you say it to yourself or someone else, doesn't it take on a distinctive rhythm and meter? Any number can acquire a rhythmic pattern all its own by simple repetition. Repeat the number 1672 five times in a row, and see what happens. Say the telephone number 472–3596 over and over until it forms a pattern in your mind.

Use Mathematical Relationships

Using simple math can provide a memory association. With some numbers, the relationship is so clear that many people automatically use their math knowledge to form associations:

- 1248 is formed by doubling each successive single digit.
- 135-5799 consists of all odd numbers in increasing steps.
- 3618 takes the first two-digit number and divides it in half.

Most numerical relationships, however, are not this simple. Some people can quickly see relationships among objects in terms of ratios, increases, decreases, and step changes. Taking the telephone number 363-2100, you could simplify it by using the anchor point of 3 and counting the number of step changes in each direction: "up 3, even, down 1, down 2, down 3." The people who use this technique often mentally "see" a step scale along with, or in place of, the word description.

Use Cultural Associations

Many numbers are naturally linked to some object, measurement process, or belief within the society. For instance, what does the number 13 immediately conjure up? Bad luck, of course. These immediate connections can be used to *substitute* for numbers in association formation. Here is a list of some additional number associations that are ready made: 2 = twin, 5 = nickel, 6 = six-pack, 7 = dwarfs, 12 = dozen, 16 = sweet, 19 = this century, 20 = a score, 21 = legal, 25 = quarter, 30 = over the hill, 36 = a yard, 44 = Magnum, 50 = states, 55 = speed limit, 65 = retire. This is not a complete listing, but only some selected examples.

Use Personal Associations

Besides culturally based associations, personal belongings and experiences can be tied to specific single- and double-digit numbers. As with the cultural connections, these can be used to create quick association substitutions for numbers. For example, I have

Numbers

been married *one* time, have *two* children, own *three* TVs, teach *four* classes per year, live *five* miles from work, and so on.

Many different personal dimensions can be used for creating number associations. Make them "stable" numbers or ones that are not likely to change. Your shoe size and birth year will not change, but the number of employees in your department or the size of your salary (you hope) will. Below is a list of possible dimensions to use for associations:

Number of physical belongings (cars, houses, fishing rods, guns)
Your age
The year of a certain event (your first job)
People in your family (siblings, cousins)
Clothing sizes (hat, waist, inseam, chest, shoe, or dress size)
Multiple events (marriages, jobs, European trips)

EXERCISE

Fill in each number from 1 to 20 with your own personal association, plus a few more from each of the other ranges. If the system works for you, create an entire range of associations from 1 to 100.

1. _____   11. _____
2. _____   12. _____
3. _____   13. _____
4. _____   14. _____
5. _____   15. _____
6. _____   16. _____
7. _____   17. _____
8. _____   18. _____
9. _____   19. _____
10. _____   20. _____

21–29 _____

30–39 _____

(CONTINUED)

40-49 _____

50-59 _____

60-69 _____

70-79 _____

80-89 _____

90-100 _____

Use Your Hobby or Personal Activities

As you may remember, there is a limit of about seven items in short-term memory before it is overloaded. In a recent investigation, several memory researchers tested whether someone could expand this limit if given enough practice. They selected an individual and presented sets of numbers to him, trial after trial after trial. At first, he couldn't push much beyond the seven-item limit, but after a while he dramatically increased the number of digits he could recall. The surprised researchers found that he eventually pushed his limit to around fifty numbers at once.

His solution was to take each number and turn it into a running time. As a serious jogger, he could easily convert a string of unrelated numbers into a race time in hours, minutes, and seconds. This allowed him to increase his capacity for remembering numbers substantially by turning them into a more personal form.

Do you have a special hobby or interest or pastime that relates to numbers? If you are a baseball enthusiast, convert numbers into batting averages. Use familiar football players' jersey numbers as substitutes. If you climb mountains for relaxation, change digits into heights of mountains.

Establish a Motor Pattern

As touch-tone telephones replace the rotary-style phones, a change has occurred in how phone numbers are stored in memory. People have developed "finger memories." With frequently dialed numbers, their hand knows what to do automatically. When first

Numbers 173

learning a number, dial it over and over again, six or seven times in a row until you get the feel of it. This will speed up the pace of this finger association and set it in memory much earlier.

Unfortunately, the world is not totally push button yet, and on occasion, people must use a rotary dial telephone to dial a touch-learned number. When this occurs, individuals are surprised to find that the phone number is stored in their hand, not in their head. This type of finger memory is not odd; skilled typists show the same thing. They can locate the letter P on the keyboard much faster with their finger than they could describe its position to you.

Although this is the Associate section, here is a quick Support technique: I have provided a diagram of a touch button phone face below. For some reason, people who designed calculators and

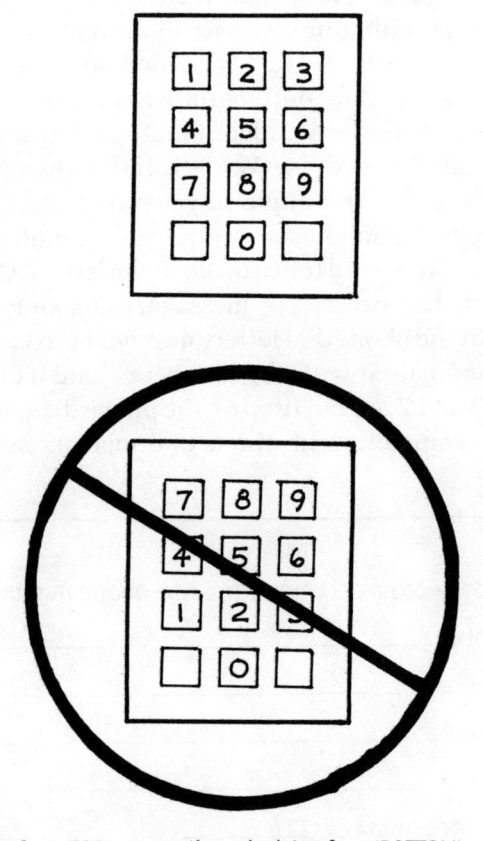

The telephone face (TOP) versus the calculator face (BOTTOM)

telephone faces took opposite approaches to numbers. Telephone numbers increase from the top down, while calculator numbers increase from the bottom up. Because most businesspersons work with both devices, it is easy to get the two confused when conjuring a mental picture of the telephone face. Tear the touch dial out and carry it with you (in your wallet, purse, or appointment book). If you run across a rotary dial phone, pull out your diagram and touch out the number on it. This will save time and may avoid interference.

Translate Phone Numbers into Words

Advertisers often use the letters on the face of the telephone rather than the numbers to help your memory. For instance, you might hear, "For expert plumbing service in the metropolitan area, simply dial P−L−U−M−B−E−R." The company's number actually is 758−6237, but spelling out "plumber" on the dial is much easier to remember. Or the local indoor tanning salon advertises in the newspaper to call T−A−N K−W−I−K rather than 826−5945.

You can also use this technique to generate your own phone number associations. When somebody gives you a number, and you are near a phone, make a word (or two) out of the letters. Companies buy numbers to fit their product or message, so making up appropriate slogans to fit the phone dial letters may not be as easy for you. There are no letters paired with the numbers 1 and 0 on the dial. Since the letters Q and Z are not used on the phone dial, pair Q with 1 and Z with 0 to complete your phone-dial memory system.

EXERCISE
Try a phone dial word association for a few phone numbers:

Home phone number _____

Office phone number _____

Friend's phone number _____

Doctor's number _____

Emergency (fire, police) number _____

☞ A STANDARD NUMBER MNEMONIC

For those who deal with numbers constantly and need to have a large quantity of ever-changing statistics readily retrievable, a more sophisticated memory technique might be useful. I *do not* recommend this technique for everyone because memorizing and perfecting its application takes considerable time and effort. And if it is not used on a regular basis, it may not stay with you. In a sense, it is like a foreign language.

Each of the ten single digits is paired with a primary consonant sound. Once you learn these associations, then you can carry out a *two-step* translation process to memorize a number string. The first step is to translate the single digits into single letters. The second step is to create a word (or two) using the letters.

First, I will explain the translation and then give you some numbers as practice material. There are no consistent principles determining the way the numbers and sounds are paired with each other. Some pairings involve a visual relationship, some a sound correspondence, and some connect via a shared word. For each pairing, I will describe the relationship between the number and the first letter listed. Since it is actually a sound-number connection, there are several additional letters that may share the same sound with the first letter, and can be used interchangeably with it. Simply learn the associations and strengthen them through repetition. In order to be effective, the associations must be very strong, so that they can be called up and applied quickly. The only way to achieve this is to practice it over and over again.

Number	Consonants	Association
1	t, d	one downstroke
2	n	two downstrokes
3	m	three downstrokes
4	r	word "four" ends with an r
5	l	hand makes L with thumb out
6	j, sh, ch, g (soft)	J and 6 are mirror images
7	k, c (hard), g (hard)	two 7s can form a K
8	f, v, ph	script f and 8 are similar
9	p, b	P and 9 are mirror images
0	z, s, c (soft)	word "zero" begins with a z

For 1, the "t" and "d" both have a single downward stroke. For 2 and 3, there are direct visual associations with the number of downstrokes in the small letters n and m. With 4 and 0, there is a *word* association: the last letter of "four" is r and the first letter of "zero" is z. There are 5 fingers in a hand, and if you hold up your left hand with the back facing you with the thumb extended to the side, this forms the shape of a capital letter "L."

Both 6 and 9 depend on reversed letter images, with a J as a backward 6 and a P as a backward 9. With 8, a script version of an f has an upper and lower loop like an 8. Finally, 7 is a bit cryptic. If you leaned one upside-down (and reversed) 7 against another upright 7, you would produce something that resembled the letter K. Use your imagination!

Once the associations are formed, the application is fun. The number "1274" can be represented by the letters t, n, k, and r. This could be quickly turned into "tanker" or "tinker." A phone number such as 523–7807 would translate into the letters l, n, m, g, f, c, and f. These letters could turn into a phrase like "a lone mug of coffee." At first, creating the words is very time-consuming, but you will get gradually better with practice. Note that for over half the numbers (1, 6, 7, 8, 9, 0) there is flexibility in which letters you use to represent the number. Some letters fit better than others for constructing certain words, so do some experimenting.

Here are a few extra rules:

1. Vowels have no value. They are only fillers.
2. The letters W, H, and Y are also ignored when they occur in a word.
3. Silent letters are disregarded: "knee" = 2, not 72.
4. Double letters count as one number: "letter" = 514, not 5114.
5. Watch the double-sound letters—c and g: the "hard" versus "soft" pronunciations will lead to different numbers.

This system is conveyed in greater detail in other popular memory books. It can be fun to use, but you must be willing to spend some time perfecting it. You should also have an opportunity for its continued and routine use or your skills will weaken.

Numbers

EXERCISE
The first exercise is for translating numbers into words, and the second for translating words back into numbers.

Number to Remember	Word or Phrase
1. 9602	_____
2. 327–8851	_____
3. 01827	_____
4. 83,902,714	_____
5. $348.77	_____
6. Your phone number	_____
7. Your house number	_____

Word or Phrase	Number Represented
1. memory	_____
2. zodiac	_____
3. juggle	_____
4. lamps	_____
5. dreadful	_____
6. delicate	_____

Since the numbers 1 through 20 are used often, you may find it convenient to generate a set of **standard** words for these numbers. I have provided some words as examples but feel free to generate your own:

1 = __toe__   6 = _____
2 = _____   7 = _____
3 = _____   8 = _____
4 = __rye__   9 = _____
5 = _____   10 = _____

(CONTINUED)

11 = _____   16 = _____
12 = ____ton_____   17 = ____dike_____
13 = _____   18 = _____
14 = _____   19 = _____
15 = _____   20 = _____

This system can be taken far beyond 20. If you need to use numbers regularly and find this system useful, I encourage you to generate your own list of personal word associations up to 100.

Incidentally, once you memorize your standard word associations, this system can also be used as a pegword system. In Chapter 13, "Lists," I mentioned that one way to keep track of a list of items is to form an intermediate word based on sound (1 = bun) or sight (1 = cane) and then form an association between the intermediate word and the list item. The same idea holds with the number-word pairs you generate here, as long as the words describe actual objects.

EXERCISE

Regardless of whether you choose the standard number mnemonic or one of the other techniques suggested earlier in the chapter, practice your number memory skills to do some of the following:

1. Learn all your credit card numbers.
2. On the freeway, memorize car license plate numbers.
3. At a restaurant, memorize the prices of the main dinners.
4. Try to remember the numbers on athletes' jerseys.
5. Remember each phone number you hear.
6. Memorize the catalog number of each item in your product line.

MEMOREVIEW: Numbers

ATTEND

Develop a positive attitude about numbers.
Determine which numbers are most important.
Go for approximations, not exact values.

ASSOCIATE

Combine numbers into pairs or groups.
Construct a mental chart.
Use a letter or word for number magnitude.
Make up phrases or rhymes for the number.
Establish a distinct auditory rhythm.
Use mathematical relationships.
Use cultural associations.
Use personal associations.
Use your hobby or personal activities.
Establish a motor pattern.
Translate phone numbers into words.

A STANDARD NUMBER MNEMONIC

17

Making a Speech

Most businesspersons have to make presentations, give speeches, or train others in a formal setting. The frequency of presentations often increases in a direct relationship with one's responsibilities.

Your first decision when you have to make a speech is whether to write it out and read it, or make an outline of key points and present the speech from memory in a more spontaneous fashion. If you choose to *read* your speech from a text, this chapter is unnecessary for you. But I would not recommend this approach, because your audience may wonder why they should remember something that the presenter isn't interested in committing to memory.

If you do decide to work from an *outline*, then you need to select and organize the key points, memorize them, and hold all the parts of the speech in memory while you're up in front of the group. Although there are a number of dimensions to successful speeches, a major part is your ability to make your memory work efficiently under the added distraction and stress of being in front of an audience. The purpose of this chapter is to address this one issue, and to enable you to present your material without the fear of forgetting what you want to say, and to be more confident and assured in your presentation.

To manage your memory for speech material, techniques to enhance your attention are not relevant. The fact that you are giving the talk is enough to keep you focused on the task and material. Therefore, only Associate, Rehearse, and Support suggestions will be presented.

☞ ASSOCIATE

For any presentation, build a skeleton outline of the presentation, using simple key words and phrases to provide the core memory structure to which supplementary points and illustrations will be attached. It is important to associate the primary points in such a way that they come back to you easily when you are giving the speech. There are three ways that this can be accomplished. One way is to connect the points to features of the external environment. A second associational strategy hooks each idea with parts of your body. Finally, you can create a mental list to follow during your talk.

Connect Points to Room Features

Several thousand years ago, a Greek orator named Simonides was giving a talk at a banquet. He was called out of the room for a moment to talk to a messenger, and while he was gone the roof collapsed, killing everyone in the audience. Most of the bodies were crushed beyond recognition, so the officials called on Simonides for help. By recalling where each person was sitting, he was able to identify each body scattered throughout the room. Simonides was so impressed with his ability to remember each person by location that he tried using locations for his speeches. He tied each of his points to a separate location around the room where he would be speaking. When it came time to give the speech, he would simply look at each successive location and the associated idea would spring back to him.

You can easily apply this system too if you are acquainted with or have access to the room ahead of time. From the front of the room, look around for distinct objects and locations: a door, a window, a picture, a coatrack, a bulletin board, etc. Connect a main point to each object, making an interacting image.

If your first point is the financial objectives of your new plan, visualize dollar bills pasted all over the door. If the second idea in your speech is the personnel reduction that your plan will necessitate, associate this with the window by seeing people jumping out of it. Make the order of the points correspond with the order of the locations. Scan the room from left to right, a natural reading order, and hook the first speech topic to the first location on the left, the second idea to the next object, and so on.

If you do not have access to the room that you will be speaking in, it is still possible to use the method of locations. Select another location that you are familiar with, such as your home or office. In the same manner that you used the actual physical setting, you can attach your ideas to locations in your mind and mentally walk back through them as you give your presentation. For more details on this technique, see Chapter 13, "Lists."

Use Body Parts and Position

One associative device that you can always count on having with you is your body. Mark Twain once tried to cue his speech by writing key words on his fingers to remind him of points. The problem was that the audience also noticed the words on his fingers, and these became as interesting as his speech.

A better use of the body is to associate mentally each point with a different *body part*. Spend a few minutes selecting the parts that you would like to use—foot, knee, elbow, ear, etc. As with the location system, make a systematic march across your body to correspond to the speech ideas. For example, start at your left foot, work up the left side of your body to your left ear and then across and down the right side.

Referring back to the speech mentioned in the last section, your first point, on finances, could be connected to your left foot by pretending that you are standing in a pot of gold coins. The second point, on personnel reductions, may be associated with your left knee by imagining tiny people fighting and grasping to hold on to your knee while trying to climb your leg.

Another technique for memorizing a sequence of speech topics is to link each one with a different *body posture* or stance. Holding on to the podium could be stance number one. Crossing your arms and moving one step to the right of the rostrum could be stance number two. Putting your hands behind your back could be stance number three. The speech becomes a choreographed sequence of standard postures. While standing in each position, practice one of the ideas. After practicing the speech with the physical movements, the presentation can come back to you, point by point, as you again assume each posture.

Make a Mental List

Chapter 13, "Lists," provides several different mental list techniques. Since a speech is framed around a mental list, it may be useful to refer to that chapter. The three basic list techniques are the chain, location, and pegword systems. I have presented the location method in detail here because its origin lies in public speaking. However, the other two techniques—chain and pegword—could also be applied to a public speaking setting.

☞ REHEARSE

Overlearn the Material

Whenever you are under stress, even a mild form, it jeopardizes the efficiency of your retrieval process. The most effective protection against stress-induced forgetting is to drill the material in, far beyond simply setting it in long-term memory. The extra repetitions seem to strengthen the retrieval routes and make them less susceptible to disruptions.

Overlearning separates the amateur and the professional. Professional actors can go through a variety of different and unexpected stage disruptions without forgetting their lines. Professional paramedics always remember the series of steps to follow for a variety of traumas, regardless of how much situational turmoil they find themselves in.

Rehearse the material far beyond what you feel is necessary. This will seal it in and provide you with memory insurance.

Do a Complete Dry Run

Hearing yourself talk through the presentation makes the material sink in even deeper. If you can present it in the actual room, this is even better. Try to include any media that you will use, such as slide and overhead projectors, handouts, and charts. On occasion, a presenter will give a speech that he or she rehearsed to proficiency in front of the mirror. Then confronted with an ornery slide projector, the speech falls apart. Practicing the motions and manipulation needed for the audiovisuals will decrease the chances that they will disrupt your presentation or memory.

Work on your gestures, movements, and body position during the run-through. The series of steps and movements that you go through while practicing will help form a thread to tie together the pieces of your talk. Have a friend sit in the audience to give you practice focusing on people. You can also get helpful feedback concerning the impact of your presentation.

☞ SUPPORT

Go to the Room Early

On the day of your talk, try to get to the room before anyone else does. Even if you are familiar with the room, getting there early helps you to ease into the setting. If you appear only a few minutes before your talk, you may have to deal with old friends, shuffled notes, a missing podium, and a misadjusted sound system all at once. This can create a state of moderate stress and confusion that could interfere with your memory retrieval efforts.

Put Cue Words on Sheets or Cards

Whatever associational scheme you use, write out a skeleton outline of your speech, consisting of one or two words to key each point. This will provide a backup to which you can refer in case you lose a point. Make the print large, with plenty of space between words so you can read it clearly several feet away. This will allow you to wander away from the podium, but still be able to glance over and read your outline. Even if you don't refer to it, it is comforting to know that you have it available. It is a presentation security blanket.

For a more elaborate support, try a *dual* cue card system. One card has the simple keyword outline. The other card has the same outline duplicated, but with filler or illustration points added.

Concentrate on the Interested Individuals

One of the best ways to boost your confidence and support your retrieval efforts is to scan the audience and talk directly to those individuals who appear to be interested and receptive to what you have to say. It is unrealistic to try to win over everybody in the room and have them nodding in agreement by the time you are through.

I still have painful memories of the first course I taught in college. It was in the Evening Division, and each night a particular student in the front row would lay his head down and fall asleep in the middle of my lecture. This was very upsetting to me at that tender point in my career, and my memory would go blank as a result. I soon learned that picking out the few attentive individuals can be the most effective way to prevent anxiety-induced memory failure.

MEMOREVIEW: Making a Speech

ASSOCIATE
   Connect points to room features.
   Use body parts and position.
   Make a mental list.

REHEARSE
   Overlearn the material.
   Do a complete dry run.

SUPPORT
   Go to the room early.
   Put cue words on sheets or cards.
   Concentrate on the interested individuals.

18

Examinations

As competition for professional services becomes more intense, and the need for training becomes more specialized, examinations are being used as a way of monitoring and ensuring professional quality. Not only are consumer groups demanding them, but the professionals themselves see testing as a means for policing their own ranks and maintaining high standards.

Ironically, our schools do not provide training on how to take tests. The naive assumption is that the knowledge, if it is there, will simply tumble out when the right memory compartment is opened up. This notion is far from reality. The ability to store a large body of systematized knowledge in memory and get it out under adverse or stressful conditions depends to a large extent on effective study strategies.

One of the primary reasons for poor performance on an examination is that the circumstances under which the material is learned differ considerably from those under which the test is taken.

Let's look at a typical exam setting. You are sitting at a desk with restricted movement and comfort, writing down the answers to questions you may never have dreamed of. The atmosphere is quiet, but somewhat stressful; there are time constraints.

Contrast this with how you studied. You were relaxed, dressed comfortably in your bathrobe, sitting in an easy chair, with a moderate level of background music or noise. As you sip a cup of coffee and munch some pretzels, you go over in your mind extensive, ordered lists of information you have stored in memory and recite them aloud.

Examinations

For most people, there is little resemblance between study and test conditions. You have practiced remembering information (studying) in a manner quite different from the way you will actually have to remember it during the test. Your mind becomes used to recalling the information in one way, and it is hard to switch it into another retrieval mode.

In this chapter, I will suggest a number of techniques for improving your performance during an examination. The tips will be aimed at storing the material efficiently, adjusting to the examination setting, and retrieving the information effectively in that setting.

☞ ATTEND

Clarify the Importance of the Test

In order to study conscientiously, it is important that you know what the benefits of the examination would be: career advancement, certification—or simply satisfying your boss. One primary reason for an inability to concentrate is the lack of a clear idea of your reasons for taking the test or what impact it will have on your life. If you are unclear about how this exam ties in with your career goals, it will be considerably more difficult to focus on it. Ask yourself, "How will I benefit from this test?" and "What difficulties could I encounter if I don't pass this exam?"

Determine What Type of Exam Will Be Given

Well before you start studying for an examination, find out as much as you can about what *type* of test it is: essay, short answer, identification, matching, word recall, or multiple choice. Research has shown that knowing the test format ahead of time significantly aids performance. If students study for one type of test (multiple choice) and are actually given another type (short answer), they do worse than if they know ahead of time what sort of test it will be.

Finding out what to expect will increase your ability to attend to the correct features of the information and remember them in the most efficient manner.

☞ ASSOCIATE

The key to successful studying is to establish a variety of memory triggers—mental and physical cues that let you pull out the correct information from memory.

Study in the Same External Context

As you study, you *actively* create mental associations to help you recall the material. But at the same time you are acquiring *passive* associations with the physical setting and your mental state. The information becomes linked with your surroundings, so that if the same environmental cues are present during study as during the test, they can help pull the information back out.

If at all possible, study for an exam in the same room that you will be taking it in. I have suggested this to my students, and those who try it claim that being in the classroom the night before seems to make the information flow more easily the next day.

However, studying in the test room may not be possible. If it is not, just imagining that you are in it when you study can help improve your performance later.

Duplicate the external environment of the actual examination as closely as you can:

Background noise. Don't study with extraneous noises or music playing in the background. Even soft music is inappropriate, unless it will be piped in during your exam.

Desk or table. Don't sit in an easy chair or at a sofa. Use a desk or table, or at least sit upright, as you will have to do during the exam.

Clothing. Study in the same clothing that you will wear during the exam. Pick out an outfit that is suitable for the exam setting, and wear it each time you study. If you have some jewelry or rings, these may also be useful to establish a consistent context, and could be used to make mental association with. Form direct associations between each major point and a particular item of clothing.

Time of day. Schedule the bulk of your studying at the same time of the day as your exam will be.

These tips are not meant to take the place of serious, effortful memorizing. They may simply boost your ability to recall the information later. For the minimal effort spent, this may make a substantial difference in a highly competitive situation.

Study in the Same Internal Context

In the same manner that information gets passively hooked to external cues, the information can also stick to "internal" cues or bodily states. Memory can be "state dependent": if you learn something under one mental state, it is easier to recall the information when you are in that *same* state, rather than a changed state.

Most of the research in this area has been done with alcohol. If you learn something when you are intoxicated, it is *easier* to recall that information later if you are intoxicated again, rather than sober, and vice versa. This does not mean that your memory will fail when your internal state changes. You will simply recall less.

Therefore, don't drink beer or wine while you are studying unless you can have the alcohol again while you take the test. The same holds true of caffeine and nicotine, both of which change your physical and mental state. If coffee is allowed during the exam, go ahead and study sipping coffee. If you are a smoker, and know you can smoke during the exam, go ahead and light up while you're studying. Otherwise, don't.

Reduce the Material to Key Words

Try to boil the material down into single words or short phrases that capture the central ideas and concepts. Form these cue words into a memory core around which to build the other information.

These cue words can then become the primary hooks to pull the material from memory.

For instance, if you had to learn *this* chapter for a later test, you could learn the topics under Attend by using the key words "motivate" and "type of test." For the Associate section, translate the points into "outside," "inside," "key words," and "lists" (below). Each of these words should be sufficient to pull the rest of the information back out.

Another helpful technique is to *layer* the material into successively higher levels, creating an information pyramid. The way this chapter is organized is an example. "Exams" at the top, "Attend, Associate, Rehearse, and Support" at the second level, each of the subpoints on the third level, and so on. Often, material is organized in this manner for you. Not only does this hierarchy make recall more efficient and ordered, but the process of mentally wrestling with the information to evolve such a structure is likely to produce stronger associations.

Use Lists

The techniques discussed in Chapter 13 can be very beneficial in studying for tests. Examination material often comes in ordered bundles or sequential groupings, and the techniques for memorizing lists are usefully applied here. Acronyms are especially helpful, and top students frequently use them. By extracting the first letters from a set of keywords and making it into an acronym, you can recapture the entire list of terms. To remember the memory system of Attend, Associate, Rehearse, and Support, you could condense it into AARS and think of yourself that this chapter is like going back to school and learning the basic three Rs, except now it is the four AARS.

☞ REHEARSE

Write It Over and Over

Practice (rehearsal) by repeated *writing* will be more effective because the exam itself will undoubtedly be written. Write the information from your memory as if you were actually taking the exam. If you are studying with a friend, copy the information that you dictate to each other. Or recopy your own notes, outline, or underlinings.

One acquaintance developed a clever twist on this technique. He would pretend that he was going to cheat on an examination. To do this, he recopied *all* his notes on one 3 by 5 card, which he would supposedly hide and try to sneak into the examination. He never actually cheated, but the extraordinary feat of condensing all his notes forced him to concentrate on and rehearse the material so thoroughly that he ended up memorizing it with ease.

Generate Possible Test Questions

After you have become fairly familiar with the material that the examination is to cover, practice making up your own test questions. Pretend that you are the person responsible for the test. Make up several different questions on each section, set them aside, and answer them later. This gives you at least two repetitions—once making up the questions and once answering them. Remember that a *person* (not a machine) makes up the test and certain types of questions are more obvious than others. When you look at the information from the perspective of the person constructing the test, you are likely to generate some actual test questions in the process.

Recruit a Study Partner

Studying can be a drudgery. Finding someone to go through it with you can make the process more enjoyable.

Compare Underlinings.

If examination material is taken primarily from a text, compare your underlinings with your partner's. Where they match, you can assume that the material is essential. Where your notations don't match, each person can explain why they consider their underlinings important. Ideally most of the discrepancies will be resolved, but in any event you will have gotten additional review of the information.

Quiz Each Other with Prepared Questions

If each of you makes up a set of questions on your own, as suggested in the last section, you can quiz each other. Try to make a good, but difficult test. The winner gets lunch from the loser.

Play Teacher and Student

If the examination material is so extensive that you will have difficulty covering it all, split it up and teach it to each other. Be the teacher for half the material and the student for the other half. Go over concepts, terms, and relationships, explaining them in detail using a tutorial technique. If you have never taught before, you will be pleasantly surprised at how well this helps you learn and remember information.

Several years ago, I began studying for a comprehensive professional exam with a study partner who was not holding up his end of the bargain. At first, I was irritated at the thought of "wasting" my time going over the material with him when he hadn't read much of it. To my surprise, I found that going over the material with him implanted it in my own mind in a stronger, clearer fashion, and my performance on the test benefited greatly from this.

Make Two-Sided Cards with Terms and Definitions

Often, the content area of a particular examination consists mainly of key terms, concepts, laws, or theories. For the examination, you have either to provide the *term* that fits a definition, or provide the *definition* of a certain term. If this is the case, construct a set of old-fashioned flash cards, with the key words on one side and the defining description on the other. Rehearse by studying the material in both directions, so that your memory retrieval works effectively both ways. Go through the definition sides and let this cue the terms. Then flip through the term sides and pull out the definitions from memory.

☞ SUPPORT

Get Plenty of Sleep the Night Before

A common practice among habitual test takers (mostly students) is cramming, or pulling "all-nighters." This may result in good stories, but also in bad memories.

When studying for a serious examination, it is imperative that you get a good night's sleep. Fatigue can hurt you in two ways. First, the material that you study as you approach exhaustion in small hours of the night will be difficult to store and hard to "find" the next day during the exam. Fatigue can also interfere with test performance. When your energy level is low, your entire body will function less well, and your memory along with it. It is more difficult to recall information when you are tired.

Learn to Cope with Temporary Memory Blocks

One of the most devastating experiences one can have while taking a test is to suffer a block, triggered by negative emotions. Nervousness, worry, apprehension, or distress can hamper your ability to recall even well-learned information. People continually come up to me after examinations, claiming that their mind went blank because they became nervous.

This problem has two primary causes. The first is general. We all experience some general anxiety before a test. Just walking into the room creates it. The other source of memory block arises during the test. As you diligently move along answering the questions, you come to an item that you block on momentarily. This causes a mild panic, which then makes you unable to recall the answers to the next few items. The anxiety feeds on itself.

To alleviate these anxiety-caused blocks, try some on-the-spot relaxation exercises. Close your eyes, take a couple of deep breaths and let them out slowly, and loosen up your jaw and neck muscles by tensing and relaxing them several times (tension seems to settle in this area). Then concentrate on the test items, rather than on how nervous you are.

Another approach is to move quickly beyond the blocked item, rather than concentrating on it. Find the next *familiar* item (not necessarily the next one). This will help you get back into the swing of the test, and may even break the block when you return to the item with which you had trouble. See Chapter 23, "Jogging Your Memory," for more hints on overcoming these temporary blocks.

Survey the Test before You Start

When you are handed the examination, skim through it completely before you start. For essay questions, write a brief outline in the margin next to each one to come back to. Determine your pacing by dividing the number of questions into the total time. Write projected times at the bottom of each page so you don't get caught short. Search for unexpected or blockbuster items so that you are not mentally jolted by them later.

If you skim some items that you are vague about, set your memory recall wheels in motion so that you will be lubricated by the time you reach this question. Also, if some information pops to mind that is not related to the particular question you are on but may pertain to a later item, write it in the margin or on the back of the test sheet so that you can refer back to it later.

MEMOREVIEW: Examinations

ATTEND
Clarify the importance of the test.
Determine what type of exam will be given.

ASSOCIATE
Study with the same external context.
Study in the same internal context.
Reduce the material to key words.
Use lists.

REHEARSE
Write it over and over.
Generate possible test questions.
Recruit a study partner.
Make two-sided cards with terms and definitions.

SUPPORT
Get plenty of sleep the night before.
Learn to cope with temporary memory blocks.
Survey the test before you start.

MANAGING OTHERS' MEMORIES

Have you ever supervised an employee who constantly forgets your directions or keeps asking the same question over and over again? Or made a presentation to a group and didn't seem able to get your point across? Do you have an important client who cannot remember your name—each time you meet, you have to reintroduce yourself?

A considerable part of the business day is spent in one of two ways: telling others who you are and what your message is . . . and **repeating** who you are and what your message is. Regardless of your position, you must communicate with other persons both inside and outside your company, and an important key to your success is how well others can remember who you are and what you say.

Having experienced and practiced the memory system in managing your own memory, you can now turn these techniques around and apply them to managing others' memories. This does not involve **teaching** them the system. But with what you know already about how memory works for you, you can provide information to others in a memory-ready format, ensuring that they successfully attend, associate, rehearse, and support what you tell them.

I have selected **four** areas where managing other persons' memories seem to be critical. The first, discussed in Chapter 19, is during introductions, where it is important that you get your name and business information across to them. Chapters 20 and 21 deal with oral communications of informal and formal varieties. Each of these situations requires different techniques for assuring that your audience, whether it be one or one hundred persons, remembers your ideas. Chapter 22 deals with written communications, or memos. It is not enough simply to write down your thoughts. A number of memory dimensions can determine the success or failure of memos.

The material in this part is similar to some presented in Chapters 8–10 and 17 ("Names," "Personal Information," "Conversations," and "Making a Speech"). But the information is reformatted so that it relates to helping the other person's memory, rather than your own. Some new tips have been added as well.

19

Introducing Yourself

During most routine introductions, you have a difficult memory management situation, both for you and for the person you are meeting. There are numerous distractions, ranging from your appearance to novel background noises and sights, to any nervousness the other person might feel. Therefore, it is best to limit yourself to getting across only two pieces of information: your name and your profession.

A special difficulty with introductions is that they are often done on the spur of the moment. The other person isn't really prepared to concentrate or to process information about you. In any case, you need to be constantly aware of the external and internal demands on the other person's memory capacity, and how this restricts his or her ability to learn about you.

Peter Olds, a manager of a software sales force, hired Mary Armstrong fresh out of an MBA program and made her the local sales representative for their city. Whereas new hirees normally took two to three years to "pay their dues," Mary was knocking the top off the sales charts in her first six months.

Peter's curiosity made him accompany the young woman on her next sales rounds, to find out how she generated so much business. On her first call, she visited one of her established client companies to make a few new contacts. As she walked through the corridors, each person she met called her by name and asked how she was.

When she sat down with her first new customer, she introduced herself as "Mary Armstrong from Eaton, and let me help you remember who I am. Imagine me in a wedding dress, for marry, with big bulging biceps, for arm strong, stuffing down my entire wedding cake, which stands for eat ton." The client laughed as Mary gestured through her self-introduction, but was obviously transfixed by her image. After this, she asked him some key questions about his business needs. She listened intently to what he said and, after a few minutes, jumped up and said that she would demonstrate to him how her software worked. His face brightened as he eagerly followed her down the hall to one of the office microcomputers.

Watching Mary at work was like observing a mind artist.

☞ ATTEND

Maintain Eye Contact

When you meet new people, they are often distracted by other people and activities around them. If they are glancing around the room, stop talking until they look back at you. Allow their attention to return before you continue. Stop talking for a moment, and the "silent pause" can get their attention focused back on you.

Make a Vocal Impact

It is especially important for the other person to hear the sound of your voice clearly and distinctly when you say your name and profession during the introduction. A common reason for not remembering a name is not having heard it in the first place. Do others sometimes ask you to repeat your name when you introduce yourself? If you have the habit of talking quietly during an introduction, you may be making yourself less memorable.

Sometimes I'll tell the person that my name is Alan Brown, without an *e*. The other person will then pause for a moment and say, "What do you mean, Brown without an *e*?" And then I'll reply that my first name is not Allen, the most common version, and my last name is not Browne, an uncommon version. In that short exchange, I have stirred up their attention to, and interest in, my name.

EXERCISE

Is there a quick comment that you could make about your own name, to direct someone's attention to it? "That's the German spelling." "Mine is with a y." "It's an uncommon spelling." Be creative. It doesn't have to be an association trick (that will come in the next section), just something that will get them to hold on to your name for a few moments.

Don't Compete with Distractions

If your conversation partner continues to be distracted, ask if he or she minds going to another room with you, where there is not so much activity.

Talking on the phone can also be difficult if the attention of the person on the other end is being distracted. Repeated hesitations indicate that distractions are present on the other end. Cut the conversation short and call back at another time, or suggest that you meet in person. Remember that you are probably wasting your time if you cannot capture and hold the other's attention.

Follow Up When Stuck in a Mass Introduction

You know the frustration of having a group of people introduced to you in an unmanageably large lump. If you happen to be one of the "masses" during a group introduction, approach the person you meet later and reintroduce yourself. Say that you know how difficult it is to catch all those names in a group, and that you wanted to meet personally. Even if he or she did happen to catch your name the first time through, this will provide a useful rehearsal of it.

Be Enthusiastic about Their Business

If you can get people to ask about your work, rather than your tending the information, they will be much more likely to remember what you do. How do you get them to ask? Be enthusiastic about *their* occupation first. Say to an airplane flight instructor that the work must be exciting and that you would like to know more about it. Ask a professional computer analyst about the exciting new trends in computer technology and how they will be shaping our lives.

After discussing themselves for a while, most people will realize that they don't have any idea what you do. In the middle of talking on about their career and accomplishments, they suddenly stop and comment, "Now wait a minute, I don't know anything about you!" Since they have actively sought information about you, they will be more interested in, pay closer attention to, and remember better what you say to them.

☞ ASSOCIATE

Give a Simple Name "Hook"

Many clever people intuitively understand how to manage others' memories for their name. They provide a simple image, rhyme, or phrase during introductions. When I first met Tony Johnson, he touched his toe and then his knee as he pronounced the two syllables of his first name. Then he said, "Johnson and Johnson bandage," still pointing at his knee. This was a marvelous image which sealed his name in my memory.

While being introduced to Kris Hart, she kissed her hand and then placed it over her heart. These action images are impressive because of the visual and motion dimensions, and it is remarkable how effective they can be to make your name more memorable.

EXERCISE
Generate a unique image for your name. Make the name image simple, one which can be given in a short phrase. Try to create a visual, auditory, and motion image in their mind at the same time. Link yourself with a famous person who shares your same name. Make up several different phrases and test them out to see which is the most effective.

Provide an Image for Your Occupation

As with name memory, it is helpful to generate a distinct but simple image for your occupation to provide others. If you are an accountant, say that you are a "pencil and visor person." Or if you are a market analyst, say that you "have the bull by the horns." Perhaps you can state that you work for Uncle Sam rather than the government. These short phrases, or quick images, go a long way toward ensuring that what you do will be remembered by the person to whom you are talking. This image can pertain to your company, your job, or both.

EXERCISE
Generate an association for your company or profession. How do others stereotype your line of work, or the organization you work for? How is it known in the civic or professional community? Use these general impressions, whether accurate or not, to implant a quick association in the other person's memory.

Be Creative with Your Name Tag

When you are given the chance to fill out your own name tag, make it distinctive: an odd writing style, a different color pen, or large lettering. Put a pronunciation guide beside or under your name. If your name is Brent Keagler with a long *a* and people are always pronouncing it with a long *e* instead, write it in phonetic form on the tag.

Draw an image of your name on the tag. Brent Hopson could put a small rabbit beside his name, and Sue Nichols could draw two five-cent pieces to the side of her name. The pictures help people form a quick visual association, and also provide an invitation to conversation about your name.

Finally, put your name tag in a different location. Habit dictates that the name badge be placed over the left side of the chest. Try putting it on the other side of your chest, or your arm, or low on your sleeve. One daring individual I met put it on his forehead. Although it seemed odd at the time, his name made a distinct memory impression.

☞ REHEARSE

Repeat Your Name in the Conversation

As you chat with another person after the introduction, he or she could easily forget your name. To help keep this from happening, repeat your own name during your conversation. If your name is George Shuster, you might say: "Whenever I say something like that my wife says 'George, you must be dreaming!'" or . . . "My boss said the other day 'George Shuster, that idea has real merit!'"

These self referrals may feel contrived, but picture yourself in the other person's shoes for a moment. If your new acquaintance has forgotten who you are, he or she may be searching for an opportunity to ask you, again, what your name is. Providing your name a second time will ensure that the other person will pay better attention to what you are saying because they will no longer be preoccupied with the problem of having to ask for your name again.

Ask What They Know about Your Profession

One way to keep a person's memory focused on your occupation is to ask what she knows about it. More often than not, the person holds a number of preconceived notions about your line of work, some of which are true and some of which are not.

Memorize a few standard jokes about your profession that you can slip into the conversation. "Did you hear the one about the traveling computer salesman?" or "How many accountants does it take to change a light bulb?"

Another way to initiate rehearsals is to ask your acquaintance if she knows anybody else in your line of work. If she answers yes, this becomes an extra associative cue to remembering what you do. When she talks later to the acquaintance who shares your line of work, your name gets one more repetition when she asks her friend if he knows you.

☞ SUPPORT

Use Your Business Cards on All Occasions

Business cards must have been invented by a memory expert because they are an ideal, portable memory support. But there are several mistakes that people make in using them.

As I mentioned in Chapter 8, "Names," pass your card out when you *first* introduce yourself, not as you part company. With the card in hand, the other person can "see" your name, use it to aid in the correct pronunciation, and jot notes on it while talking to you. It also protects you against forgetting to pass it out when you leave.

Don't limit the number of cards you pass out. If you run into a client again, don't ask if he or she has a card—simply provide another one. The more of your cards the person has, the more likely he or she will run across one when needed.

Write information about yourself on your business card during your introduction. Indicate how your name should be pronounced or provide the phone number where you can be reached on your upcoming ski vacation. Writing on the card draws the other person's attention to the card, makes the information more alive and active, and increases the chances that it will make a distinct impression on the other's memory.

Cards are such a convenient support that some people use "personal" cards, a simplified version of the business card containing only their name, address, and phone number. These can be given to the mechanic when you take your car in for service, or attached to your watch when you take it in to the repair shop. This saves your having to wait while the service person asks you for information for the claim form.

EXERCISE

Evaluate the memory impact of your business card. When you hand it out, do people comment on it, or do they tuck it away without a second glance? It is nice to have a dignified business card, but you may be missing a golden opportunity to make yourself more memorable. A distinctive symbol, color, typeface, or word spacing may make a more lasting impression.

Follow Up a Few Days Later

After meeting someone, send something with your name and occupation on it a few days later. This can be an informal letter or small gift—a notebook, a pen, or a calendar with your name and business printed on it. Send these memory supports a few days after you meet someone. Don't wait for special occasions and holidays to pass them out as gifts—you may have been forgotten by then. The important part of these follow-ups is to get your name in front of the person, again, in a concrete form.

MEMOREVIEW: Introducing Yourself

ATTEND
    Maintain eye contact.
    Make a vocal impact.
    Don't compete with distractions.
    Follow up when stuck in a mass introduction.
    Be enthusiastic about their business.

ASSOCIATE
    Give a simple name "hook."
    Provide an image for your occupation.
    Be creative with your name tag.

REHEARSE
    Repeat your name in conversation.
    Ask what they know about your profession.

SUPPORT
    Use your business cards on all occasions.
    Follow up a few days later.

20

One-to-One Messages

Everybody has experienced the frustration of carefully explaining something to someone and finding out later that the person does not remember what you said. You can put your newly acquired understanding of memory function to work to fine-tune the way you provide information to others. This chapter will cover informal conversations of a relatively private nature. The next chapter will cover more formal presentations or speeches. The main difference between the two approaches is the degree of preparation and the size of the audience. This chapter is a companion to Chapter 10, "Conversations."

☞ **ATTEND**

Allow Time for the Person to Make a Mental Transition

When you start a conversation with someone, whether in person or by phone, never assume that you have his or her full attention. Warm up with some personal chitchat before getting to your point. If you are on the phone, *always* ask whether the person you are calling is free to speak to you, and not in the middle of something else. If the answer is no (explicit or implied), *call back*. You'll get only divided attention if the person at the other end of the call is distracted. Don't try to squeeze in a quick message: "Well, this will just take a second...." or "Let me just say this and get off the phone...." It doesn't work.

This caution also applies to face-to-face conferences. Even when a conference has been scheduled in advance, the other person may have difficulty putting a current task aside. Always begin your conference by asking what the person is working on. If your associate plunges immediately into an animated description, you need to expend some effort to pull him away from this involving task and over to what you have to say.

When you are sure that you have the other person's undivided attention, don't immediately jump into your message. Allow time for him to adjust to the conversation. This is an ideal time to ask about any personal events which you remember about him (see Chapter 9, "Personal Information").

Vary the Pace and Intensity of the Message

Even if you have a fascinating message, people need variety to keep them awake and attentive. Be sure to vary your tone of voice and your pacing. Pause frequently and ask if there are questions. Interject comments, stories, or illustrations as often as possible. Take short stretch breaks. Call on the other person to share his or her experiences on the topic.

☞ ASSOCIATE

Honor the Other's Personal Memory Style

If you communicate with an individual on a regular basis, determine what that person's strong and weak sensory modalities are. If they are auditory, discuss the message in detail, embellishing it with stories and anecdotes. Encourage your hearer to interrupt you with his or her own comments.

If the person you are talking to happens to be visually oriented, have a note pad or a chart nearby or try to hold the conversation where there is a blackboard. Draw plenty of diagrams and pictures. As you bring up important terms and concepts, write them down.

For motion-oriented people, allow their contribution to the presentation when possible. Use your hand gestures freely to supplement your descriptions, and relate your ideas to their own experiences. And don't require that they sit still throughout your entire conversation.

In one seminar, after I presented the sensory modality memory style differences, a district manager and his supervisor approached me independently. They had both experienced a startling revelation during the seminar. In the past, the supervisor continually called the district manager with instructions, but received little response. Even flying to the office and having direct conferences seemed to be of little help. In contrast, the district manager constantly sent written memos to his supervisor, and most of the time they seemed to be ignored. They both realized now that they were using *their* own memory styles for communication—and achieving little result. Their communications were not being consciously resisted or ignored, but were simply not having any impact.

In many one-to-one communications, you may not have the time or ability to determine the other's memory style. In these situations, vary your message to include all the styles. Make each of your points *three* ways: say it, visualize it, and demonstrate it.

Involve Your Listener Directly

Several years back, I met a departmental manager who was very successful in one-to-one conversations. Not only were people eager to talk with him, but they seemed to remember much of what he had to say.

His technique was elegantly simple. Before he asked about a new policy change, he would say, "Now, you tell me, how many years have we had the old policy?" If there was a problem with an employee that he wanted your advice on, he would ask, "You've handled some touchy interpersonal situations, haven't you?" or "Haven't you known this person for four or five years? What is your impression of her?" Sometimes the comments were of a more general nature:

"You're a smart person, so what would you do?"
"You have had experience in this before."
"This sounds like something you would be good at."

The procedure was simple, but effective. Before beginning the conversation, he would make sure that his listener was personally involved or was invited into the process. Even when this manager engages in a monologue, the people with him feel that they are actively involved.

Use a Doodle Pad

The note pad can work both ways in memory management for conversation. Not only can it aid your memory, it can also provide associations for the person with whom you are talking. When I talk with a client or a student, I put a note pad between us and write down each point as I make it.

This provides a focal point for the conversation, as well as a medium for creating a visual association. When one of my points is unclear, the person can point directly to it and ask for an explanation. There is no ambiguity about what point is being referred to.

The note pad also provides a memory support. When the conversation is over, I tear the sheet off my tablet and give it to the other person.

☞ REHEARSE

Encourage Others to Restate Your Points

Most courses on effective communication suggest that you restate points in order to ensure that a message was accurately received. Periodically encourage the person you are talking with to summarize what you have just said. Even if you feel certain that everything has been understood, repeating will help to seal it in your listener's long-term memory. Finally, at the end of your conference ask the other person for what he or she feels to be the three or four main points covered in your discussion.

Follow Up Later in the Day

At the end of each day, touch base again with each person you have talked to during the day. Before you leave the office, make a round of phone calls to the individuals with whom you have had important discussions. Ask them if they have had any further thoughts on your conversation or if any points are hazy, now that they have had a chance to think about them. Slip in a quick restatement of your points during the call. "After thinking it over, do you still think that the three ideas, [x], [y], and [z], make sense?"

SUPPORT

Give Your Listener a Written Summary of Your Discussion

Summarize your conversation in writing immediately after you are finished, including agreements, decisions, and tentative plans. Do this while you are with the other person, or record the comments and decisions after the person leaves. In either case, be sure that he or she gets a copy. This can prevent miscommunication, and provide support as well.

MEMOREVIEW: One-to-One Messages

ATTEND
Allow time for the person to make a mental transition.
Vary the pace and intensity of the message.

ASSOCIATE
Honor the other's personal memory style.
Involve your listener directly.
Use a doodle pad.

REHEARSE
Encourage others to restate your points.
Follow up later in the day.

SUPPORT
Give your listener a written summary of your discussion.

21

Your Audience

At Consolidated Paper Products, the latest upper-management thrust was toward continued education for its employees. To help accomplish this goal, the company contracted with the Taylor Training Institute to send future leaders through a week-long series of seminars on management training. Susy Flaxon was thrilled to be chosen for this select group, but was not looking forward to going "back to school" for two weeks. She had always had difficulty attending to lectures during college and anticipated that the forthcoming class would be just as difficult for her.

At the end of the first full day of presentations, Susy suddenly realized that she had gone through the entire day and had not faded away or lost interest once. In fact, she had learned a great deal in what seemed like an effortless manner. Was this a fluke, or did the Taylor trainers know some magic? The second day was the test, however. The lecture was to be on finance, an area which she knew nothing about, and had little interest in.

Again, she was amazed at the end of the day. Susy found that in spite of her prejudices, she became deeply involved with the lecture and ended up interested in finance! Day after day, the institute opened new doors of interest for her. And she was not alone in her amazement. All her colleagues seemed to be absorbing and remembering information at a remarkable rate.

Whether a presentation is memorable or not may depend as much on the *style* of the presenter as on the *content* of what is being presented. How often have you become excited over an ordinarily dull subject because of the way the person lectured? Or has your natural enthusiasm on a topic been blunted after a boring and tedious presentation of it?

Some people seem to have a natural ability to convey information to a group. These "master" lecturers understand how to keep an audience's attention focused and serve up the material in a mentally lubricated format that is effortlessly memorable.

In a formal presentation, it is essential to capture the audience and hold it fixed on your message. The next most important job is to package the information so that it is received with affirmative nods of the head rather than blank expressions. It is a difficult task, because you must manage many individuals' memories at one time.

In Chapter 17, "Making a Speech," I discussed ways to memorize your information so that it will be easy to recall during the speech. In this chapter, I will cover the other side of this coin—how to ensure that *they* will remember what you say.

☞ ATTEND

Discover and Eliminate Distracting Habits

Several years ago, I went to a lecture by a world-renowned psychologist. I had looked forward to it with eager anticipation. Perhaps his speech was full of valuable insights. Unfortunately, I never found out because he repeatedly took my attention away with a rather unusual arm gesture. Several times a minute, he would bend his right arm to a 90-degree angle, lean slightly to the right and thump his hip with his elbow. This gesture was so bizarre that it held me transfixed. I was absorbed with trying to figure out its origins or significance. As you may have guessed, I got nothing from the lecture except how to distract an audience.

Your audience will focus on and follow the *most interesting* thing going on during the presentation. Unfortunately, that may be some little distracting habit that you're not aware of, rather than what you are saying.

These bad habits can be *vocal:* clearing one's throat, saying "uh," talking too fast. Or they can be *behaviors:* odd arm gestures, fiddling with some object on the rostrum or with your hair or something that you are wearing. Most of these difficulties are relatively easy to overcome if you can get a critique from your friends in the audience, or by consulting a professional speech coach.

Don't assume that you have no distracting habits. Nearly everybody does. The question is, how distracting are yours?

Control Presentation Anxiety

Anxiety before giving a talk is natural, and occurs in even the most seasoned speakers. Some moderate anxiety may even help you get "up" for the talk. But if your stress level becomes excessive, it can be a major factor in distracting your listeners. The audience can usually detect stress in a speaker's voice or by his or her trembling hands. Whether the people in the audience feel sympathy or irritation, their attention will be pulled away from the message and toward the speaker's discomfort.

If you experience this difficulty when in front of a group, try taking deep breaths and letting them out slowly, or concentrating on relaxing your neck and shoulder muscles by successively tightening and letting them go loose. Conjure up the image of a calm scene—a green meadow under a blue sky—just before you give your talk. If your problem is more serious, you may want to learn self-hypnosis.

Get the Audience into a Listening Mood

Before starting on a talk, warm up the audience for listening. Engage in some informal banter with them, or tell them a story or joke. People need to get used to the sound of your voice, your accent, and your pacing. If you make an important point at the very start of your talk, the audience may not process it fully because they are still reacting to *the way you sound*.

Before your talk, select somebody to sit at the back of the room and give you a sign, such as scratching an ear, if you are not speaking loud enough. Don't ask the audience, as a group, if everyone can hear. They may be too polite and tell you that you cannot be heard in the last few rows.

Keep the Audience Off Guard

Attention thrives on variety. When the pace and intensity of your presentation remain the same, boredom sets in and people tune out. Some speakers mistakenly believe that all they have to be is loud. The audience will eventually drift away from a loud voice just as it will from one that is too soft—it will just take them longer. It is important to vary your vocal level and intensity. Keep the audience on edge. Don't lull them with your delivery and allow their senses to expect what will come next.

Use silent pauses to your advantage. Inexperienced speakers worry that if they pause too long, they might lose their audience. But a pause is actually an effective attention-grabbing technique. A hush falls over the crowd and all eyes and ears are directed toward the speaker.

Movement is also essential for holding the attention of an audience. Move freely from one side of the stage to another to give the motion-oriented members some essential stimulation. In a less formal setting, go into the audience—walk down an aisle. By walking into the midst of the crowd, you can break up the distancing effect of the podium and make the event more real and active to them.

Coax Them into Participation

Generate clever ways to encourage your audience to participate in your presentation. A group of individuals who feel involved in a process will be more likely to pay attention to and remember what went on. In a small audience, have all persons give their comments and opinions as you go around the conference table. In larger audiences, invite voluntary participation or comments at *any* time during your talk. "Plant" a friend in the audience with some comments to make on early parts of the speech. Other ways to generate participation involve taking a vote by a show of hands, having people classify themselves into various groupings, or having the audience members select discussion partners.

A trick that I occasionally pull is to make an incorrect statement or put an intentional error on the board. This usually catches several members of the audience, and breaks the ice for additional participation. The others are then tuned into a more critical analysis of the information I provide, making their attention more assured.

Relate Jokes and Anecdotes to Key Points

Several memory researchers were interested in comparing students' memories for two different types of lecture material: the main topics, and tangential jokes or anecdotes. As you may have guessed, the students recalled the jokes better than they did the academic material.

The lesson from this memory research is that if you tell a joke or cute story in the middle of your presentation, *make it relevant*. Tie it in directly to the point that you are making, rather than having it be an unrelated side comment to wake up the audience. Otherwise, they may remember your joke at the expense of your main ideas.

Show Your Enthusiasm about the Material

All emotions are contagious. It is difficult to be around someone who is laughing without getting tickled yourself. When somebody is distraught and weeping, it is hard to avoid becoming sad.

If you are excited about what you are discussing in front of the group, the audience will pick this up and get interested as well. A few exaggerations won't hurt:

"You may not believe this next point!"
"See if you are as surprised as I was about this issue!"
"I'll give you a money-back guarantee that this next idea works."

Preface your important points with mystery and excitement.

☞ ASSOCIATE

Show Your Listeners Where You Are Headed

Always have an outline of your presentation in front of your audience: a written handout, an outline on the blackboard, or a slide projected on a screen. Show where you are heading and what points you will be making next. The outline provides visually minded people with exactly what they need most—a general framework to form associations with.

This way, the audience won't miss what you are saying while trying to figure out where you are heading. It also helps those people whose minds wander momentarily during a lecture to get their attention quickly back on track.

Direct Questions to the Audience

Hearing information from several different sources will enrich the potential associations for your audience. After a lecture or seminar, audience members frequently remember specific comments or personal experiences shared by members of the audience. The contrasting auditory input from different people builds distinct memories.

Asking questions of the audience is the easiest way to achieve this variety. Don't be vague and ask, "Is everything clear?" or "Do you have any questions?" Stop periodically and direct very pointed questions at your listeners: "Can any of you guess how these last two points would create a problem for the accounting department?" or "How many million do you think they saved after they implemented this waste reduction plan?"

Use Actual or Imaginary Visual Illustrations

As I mentioned above, using visual illustrations during a presentation helps your audience form visual associations to what you are saying. If appropriate, use illustrations from two or three visual sources. A handout, an outline on a blackboard, *and* examples projected on a screen will reinforce each other, and increase the probability that your listeners will form some visual associations.

Several media mistakes are made by speakers. One is incompletely explaining illustrations. Some speakers shy away from complete explanations for fear of insulting the audience, assuming that an illustration's meaning is self-evident. They don't appreciate that people like to see and hear the information simultaneously. It makes a deeper associational imprint.

Visual aids are also mishandled by going through them too rapidly. If you flip to the next chart or slide before fully explaining the previous one, people will remain puzzled and distracted. While the audience is attempting to sort out the last graphic, they miss your current one.

An extreme version of this is the technique of multislide presentation, where numerous images are flashed on a screen in rapid succession to upbeat music. It takes about a second for our brains to identify and sort out even simple visual scenes. Blitzing an audience with a rapid succession of pictures allows little information to get through to permanent memory.

If you are unable to use visual supplements for some reason, you can still draw pictures in the heads of your audience. As you talk about a new headquarters building under construction, generate in the listeners' heads a crisp visual scene of how it looks. Include a description of textures, colors, and sizes. Give the office layout. Walk through the building with them, describing it as you go. Present your visual images slowly, so that your audience has time to build their own mental version from your description. Remember that they may not be as skilled as you are at imagining.

Generate Catch Phrases or Acronyms

Try to condense the theme of your talk into a phrase or even a made-up word. If your presentation is on new high-yield investment opportunities, you might create the phrase "emerging investibles" and repeat it throughout your talk. Or a presentation on people management could be punctuated by three styles of dealing with employees: people positives, people neutrals, and people negatives.

If you can boil down your presentation into a couple of key words, generate an acronym, using the first letters of a set of words to form a new word. A few years ago, we had the WIN campaign under President Ford—Whip Inflation Now. Even if the plan didn't work, the slogan did.

The five points in your presentation on stress management concern diet, emotions, exercise, drugs, and sleep. Arrange them into the acronym DEEDS. Play off this word in your talk, noting that you are doing good DEEDS for your body by reducing stress. This one central memory hook will enable your audience to remember all five points better.

Relate to Your Listeners' Experiences

Before any major presentation, find out some common characteristics about the members of the audience to relate your ideas to. If they all work for the same company, what are some distinctive traits: quality circles, a championship softball team, or the unruly annual picnics? This is similar to political candidates having a colorful comment or two about every city they speak in.

If the members of the audience know each other, identify one or two distinctive individuals in the group. Keying some comments toward them will make the talk more relevant to the group.

Another technique to get people involved is to tell them that you have some important information to provide, but they will have to help figure out how it best relates to their own work. You are in the position of sharing information, rather than imposing it on them. They are given partial responsibility for the success of the presentation, which will lead to stronger personal associations.

Give Several Breaks

Whenever you receive a substantial amount of information, the data presented *first* is remembered best. This is known as the *primacy effect* and is a very consistent finding in memory research. This means that what you say at the *start* of your speech is most likely to have a memory impact. But it also suggests that you can create several more "starts" if you give breaks during your speech. These pauses can take a variety of forms, from a slide tray change to a stretch break.

After each pause, your memory treats the next material as a new beginning, making it more memorable. So create several breaks during your talk, and be sure to slip in the most important information at the beginning of each section of your presentation.

☞ REHEARSE

Repeat Key Points Three Times

Advertisers understand the magic number *three*. Many routine ads will repeat the product name three times. Give your own audience the same advantage by presenting your ideas at least three times: in the introduction, during the heart of the talk, and in the summary.

Ask Questions Frequently

I have mentioned questions in the Attend and Associate sections, but they are also important for rehearsals. When you toss out a question to the audience, it lets you repeat and reemphasize a point in question form.

Questions also help the audience single out important points, and direct them back to critical information that they may have missed the first time through. Last, questions provide a pause in your delivery that allows people time to repeat to themselves the information you have just covered.

Always Summarize at the End

Never end a presentation without providing a quick review of what you have said. A conclusion is not sufficient. Make it a simple, point-by-point restatement of the main ideas. Have a distinct break in your presentation before your summary so your listeners can prepare themselves mentally for their last chance to process what you are saying.

☞ SUPPORT

Provide a One-Page Summary of Your Talk

The best support for your presentation is a single-page condensation in outline or paragraph form. This may be provided before or after your talk, or even sent along later. The most important feature is simplicity. If the information is on a single page, individuals are more likely to keep it, file it, and refer back to it.

MEMOREVIEW: Your Audience

ATTEND
Discover and eliminate distracting habits.
Control presentation anxiety.
Get the audience into a listening mood.
Keep the audience off guard.
Coax them into participation.
Relate jokes and anecdotes to key points.
Show your enthusiasm about the material.

ASSOCIATE
Show your listeners where you are headed.
Direct questions to the audience.
Use actual or imaginary visual illustrations.
Generate catch phrases or acronyms.
Relate to your listeners' experiences.
Give several breaks.

REHEARSE
Repeat key points three times.
Ask questions frequently.
Always summarize at the end.

SUPPORT
Provide a one-page summary of your talk.

22

Memos

The central problem with memos is one of quality, not quantity. The major mistake in memo production is to assume that more communication means better communication. One well-constructed memo can have more memory impact than two or three redundant or poorly constructed notes. There are a number of "format" issues concerning a written document which can influence how well the information is received and remembered. A memo should seem inviting to read, simple to understand, and personally relevant.

Many people need to be coaxed into reading. In school, reading was often treated as a drudgery, and even used as a form of punishment on occasion. As adults, "reader's block" can occur when confronted with a multipage, single-spaced communication. Tackling it seems like an immense chore, so it gets put off and set to one side.

Another reason for memory problems with memos stems from unclear writing. Memos are often poorly written, and when you get to the end of a memo, you often have no idea what point was being made.

A final difficulty arises when memos are used as a substitute for the "human touch." Some administrators use memos as much to avoid interacting with people as for communication. If employees come to view the memo as a leadership sidestep, they actively ignore them. Memos should be used to supplement direct, one-on-one communication rather than to substitute for it.

☞ ATTEND

Use Memos Sparingly

If memos are sent out too frequently they lose their attention-grabbing impact. Avoid sending memos out on a regular timetable, such as every Monday, Wednesday, and Friday. People will begin to feel that this is a formality, with little substance, like a handshake greeting, and begin to read them superficially if at all.

People who are strongly auditory- or motion-oriented will find written documents difficult to absorb. Memos should only be part of a comprehensive communication plan that also involves personal demonstration and one-to-one conversation.

Put Each on a Single Page

If it can't go on one page, it shouldn't be a memo. Confronting a single typed page seems easy, but facing a multipage document seems like much more work. Most report-like memos really could go on one page, except for the filler material or examples. If there are a number of subpoints and intricate arguments to be presented, outline them in the single-page cover sheet and refer the reader to the attached supplementary pages, which go into greater detail. On occasions where you have more than one page of information to convey, turn it into several different memos distributed at different times.

Use Plenty of Space

When constructing a written document, don't be economical with space. Paper is cheap, but losing your reader can be costly. Spread out the information as much as possible, leave white space (open areas) whenever you can. This frames the message, relaxes the eyes, and invites the reader. Use double spacing, if possible. The point of spreading out the material is to make the document more appealing to read in the first place, and easier to follow. In the same way that a framed picture is easier to look at, a word framed with blank (white) space is easier to process and remember.

Grab Your Readers in the First Sentence

To establish reader interest at the start, make the first sentence have impact. Arouse their curiosity, ask a key question, tell them what they will get out of the communication, or dare them. Here are some samples:

"Reading this may or may not make you rich."
"Know what a Q.F.R.S. is? Well, don't stop now."
"If you were thinking about throwing this memo away, don't!"
"I'm only going to make three simple points in this memo."
"Is your job on the line if you don't read this memo? No, but ..."

Be as creative or goofy as you need to be to have your readers dive in with a positive attitude.

Intrigue Your Readers

If something is hidden, forbidden, or takes more effort to obtain, it will heighten our interest in it. So try some gimmicks for the sake of attention and memory. Which would be more inviting to read if you found it in your mailbox?

An unfolded memo or a folded one?
A plain memo or one in an envelope?
A plain envelope or one with the word "confidential" on it?

The more the memo appears hidden or mysterious, the more it will capture the reader's attention. Here are some additional variations on the standard memo:

Have each person come by your office and pick up the memo.
Use a Mailgram for delivery, on special occasions.

Put it on the office computer; employees receive the message as they log on.

Put it on colored paper.

☞ ASSOCIATE

Remember the Modal Languages

The function of a written message is to plant something that will take root in the mind of the reader. You don't want just to *convey* the information, but to have your people *remember* it. Keep in mind that each sensory channel has a different language.

Visual Language. This involves words describing scenes or visual images. Preface the description with a phrase such as, "Can you see this?" "It looks like . . ." or "Picture this for a moment." These phrases help make the visual readers receptive to forming their own word pictures.

Auditory Language. The ear sense can be activated by phrases that are sound words. "Hear me out on this," "This sounds like a good start," or "I'll be listening for your input."

Motion Language. To get the most from the motion person, provide action or movement words in the memo: "This plan has a real punch," "We need to attack this problem," or "Let's move off dead center on this debate." Images that vicariously excite the muscles and move mentally through events and experiences will grab the motion person every time.

EXERCISE

Examine the last few memos that you wrote. What language style do you use? Does it consist of only one sensory style, or do you use several?

Make a directed effort to incorporate a broader range of word types. Look at other people's memos for ideas. What type of language do they use? Expand your awareness of your word phrase options to improve the impact of your communications.

Ask Questions, Leave Loose Ends, and Request Involvement

The information in a memo will have greater staying power if it is not wrapped up in a neat, tidy, closed-ended package. Leave your readers "hanging" in some way, or invite discussion, input, or feedback. A message that does not shut off discussion or further options will stick in memory better. When you describe a new office policy, ask what impact your readers think it will have. Whether or not you answer the question in the memo is not as important as making the reader wonder about, or get involved with the information.

Provide a one- or two-question survey at the end of a memo, or on an attached sheet that can be torn off and returned. Or ask that each person drop by your office in the next few days to provide his or her comments. Give the readers a chance to react to new policies, economic changes, or products and services. Even if you don't actually need their feedback, the involvement will enhance their association.

Limit Yourself to Three or Four Points

The limit of the brain's immediate information-processing capacity is about seven items. In your memos, aim for less than that so that you can be *sure* that your points have sufficient short-term processing room to make it to long-term memory.

On occasion, you will need to convey many different, and important, items. When you have more than three or four points, break them into smaller packages, or multiple memos. An overhaul in the accounting procedures will necessitate twenty five changes. Divide this information into five or six different *categories* of changes, and make a separate memo for each. "Today's memo deals only with changes in travel expense accounts under the new accounting system." In a few days, distribute another document outlining the new procedures for handling refunds and rebates.

Use Summary Symbols for Content

Put a simple visual symbol, diagram, or sketch on the top of the memo to summarize the contents. This will provide visualizers with an immediate association. If there is a meeting at 2:30 Thursday, put the calendar week across the top with a clock face reading 2:30 in the middle of the Thursday box. When the memo concerns the Christmas holiday, sketch a Christmas tree at the top. This technique makes a memo less forbidding, alerts the readers to the purpose before they begin, and gives them a ready-made association.

If your artistic talents leave something to be desired, buy a cartoon sketch book containing ready-drawn symbols and cartoon figures that you can trace over. Simple graphics can also be used to track several memos in a series. Say you have five successive memos on your impending merger with a larger company. Put five boxes at the top of each memo and insert a checkmark in one additional box as you address each new issue in a successive memo.

☞ REHEARSE

Repeat Points Several Times

As the old saying goes, "Tell them what you are going to say, say it, and then tell them what you've said." Begin each memo by stating what you want to say, then elaborate on your message in the body of the memo, and close by summarizing what you have said.

Occasionally, people complain that this repetition seems to patronize the reader. After all, intelligent people need to be told only one time. My reaction is that memory works best with repetition, and the only time that repeating a point becomes offensive is when you self-consciously draw attention to the fact: "As I told you several times already . . ." or "For the third and final time, let me say that . . ."

Provide Previews and Reviews

If you have *several* memos to distribute on a particular topic, use the beginning of each one to *review* quickly what the last memo covered and at the end briefly *preview* what the next one will cover.

If you have twenty different points to convey to your employees, this is too much to cram into one memo. But the danger in spreading it over three or four is that your readers will forget the first points when they receive later memos.

At the start of each additional memo, provide a cumulative listing of the points covered in all prior memos. At the end, preview *only* those ideas that will be covered in the next memo. This spreads out rehearsals in an easily digestible manner.

☞ SUPPORT

Make It Easy to File or Post

One organization that I belong to provides each member with a three-hole notebook when you join. At each meeting, the officers pass out an agenda that is sized and punched to fit in the notebook. You feel obligated to bring your notebook to the meeting and insert your pages, since someone has done the support work for you.

You could organize your memos in the same manner. Consider putting a coded label at the top of each of your memos, including date and topic. Provide the persons receiving your memos with file folders labeled to correspond to your memo code. How about different colors of paper for each different memo topic? Try to make filing memos more like a game and less like a chore. Even if you don't customize the pages for your recipients, don't give out oversized (or undersized) memos that are hard to file. This makes it more likely that they will get thrown away instead.

MEMOREVIEW: Memos

ATTEND
Use memos sparingly.
Put each on a single page.
Use plenty of space.
Grab your readers in the first sentence.
Intrigue your readers.

ASSOCIATE
Remember the modal languages.
Ask questions, leave loose ends, and request involvement.
Limit yourself to three or four points.
Use summary symbols for content.

REHEARSE
Repeat points several times.
Provide previews and reviews.

SUPPORT
Make it easy to file or post.

FINISHING TOUCHES

23

Jogging Your Memory

Regardless of how proficient your memory ability becomes, there will be times when you will be temporarily unable to recall certain information that you are sure you know. As with all your body systems, there are times when your brain will malfunction momentarily. While research in memory has demonstrated that these lapses are unavoidable from time to time, research has also shown that there are some simple ways to help get around these difficulties.

Do Not Panic

You have an important presentation to make to your boss, a valued client, or a group of people. As you are making your pitch, you miss a point or say something incorrectly. This flusters you, and the next thing you know you have forgotten the point you were making or the next few ideas. As you struggle to regain your mental composure, your memories seem to become only more elusive.

Although panic and anxiety are common contributors to sudden memory loss, any emotional strain can block your ability to remember even simple facts. Stories abound about people in emergency situations who forget even simple facts such as their phone number or where they were going before the accident. During an intense argument or after winning a prize, one is more likely to forget some things no matter how well they have been learned.

In such a situation, becoming upset over forgetting or trying to force the information out will only make matters worse. Try to relax: Close your eyes and take a few deep breaths. Patience will pay greater memory dividends than a direct attack.

This problem is often found in older persons who are afraid that they are losing their memory. They forget a name or where they have put something, and this causes them to become anxious, which in turn makes remembering even more difficult. Soon they completely distrust their own memory abilities and become stuck in a cycle of self-doubt and memory blockage. The source of the problem is within the people themselves, and a little relaxation can provide a quick cure.

Focus Away

Here is another common experience: You *try* to recall a specific fact—a name, a company, or a product. Although you can't think of it at the moment, it is on the tip of your tongue. The harder you try, the more elusive it seems to become. After you decide to give up and turn to another activity, the information pops into mind. Your mind seemed to have gone on searching for the fact without your active guidance.

When this happens to you, don't try to hang on and wring the word out of your brain. If you are in the middle of a conversation, move along to another topic; give your mind time to locate the information on its own. If you feel you must cover, say, "Oh well, I'm sure it will come to me in a moment," or "I know Bob's last name— just give me a moment." Phrase your statement in a positive fashion.

This type of temporary memory unavailability is embarrassing only if you make it so. When you experience the first signs of a block, let go and move on. If you are alone working on a project, pick up another task to let the information surface by itself.

If you happen to be talking in front of a group and some information slips your mind, create a small "diversion" while you search for it: Pause for a drink of water, search your pockets for a pencil, shuffle through your notes, or take out your handkerchief and wipe your forehead. Then have your audience help you out: "Now where was I heading?" "What was that last point?" Often, they will take advantage of your pause to ask questions and contribute their own comments, allowing you time to search your mind.

Back Off from a Wrong Guess

You are trying to think of the capital of North Dakota and you come up with Birmingham. Although you know that is incorrect, it keeps knocking around in your mind as you search for the correct answer. An incorrect guess can lock you into the wrong area of memory. If this happens, actively push the wrong answer out of your mind and start fresh.

I recently lent one of my books, and then needed it back again. My first thought was that a student had borrowed it. For several days, I repeatedly ran through the names of all the students I could possibly have lent it to, but could not come up with anyone. I finally decided to back out of this blind alley, and start from the top. Almost immediately, it came back to me. I had lent it to a colleague on the faculty, not to a student. Remaining locked into an incorrect memory area hampered my search, and correct retrieval of the information was easily accomplished by stepping back and starting over.

Search Each Memory File Drawer

When you bump into somebody in a setting that is different from the usual one, it may be difficult to remember his or her name. You have met the company president's spouse three times in formal attire at the annual company dinner. Then you run into the same person at the local grocery store, and you simply can't get to the name.

When this happens, spend a moment trying to recall where you usually see this person. Mentally scan your memory for the different settings you work in, or recent events you have been involved with, and you may be able to come up with the name through the "back door" by getting a *piece* of the memory as a clue. Or go through the standard *wh* questions to coax the information out: what occasion, when was it, where was it located, etc. As another approach, ask, "Now, when was the last time we saw each other?" They may fill in the clue to help you out of an awkward situation.

Another common memory "failure" experience is a vague feeling that you should be doing something at the moment but can't remember what. When this occurs, carry out a systematic search of the different categories of your activities. Is it a work activity: meeting, conference, client call-back? Or is it a nonwork activity: friend, church, sport, civic group, family? Quickly flip through the various categories of activities, and when you hit on the right category, the memory may come to you.

Go through the Alphabet

When you have the luxury of a few minutes to work on remembering some information, go through the letters of the alphabet slowly, one at a time. Quite frequently, the name or term will jump back when you hit on the correct letter.

Alphabetic cuing can be applied in several ways. For auditory persons, go through the letters aloud by saying them one at a time. Visually directed individuals can mentally imagine each letter in succession. One acquaintance of mine carries a small card in his wallet with the alphabet printed on it because he has an easier time jogging his recall when he can see the letters in front of him. Finally, motion-sensitive people can draw each letter on the palm of their hand or write the letters on a piece of paper.

EXERCISE
Using one of the following procedures, keep going until you hit a term or name which you know but can't think of at the moment. Then run through the letters of the alphabet in order. Give the technique a fair test by trying it on several blocked items.

1. Name all the people in your office or your neighborhood.
2. Answer questions from a trivia game.
3. Have someone read dictionary definitions, and supply the word.

Be Logical

We all behave in very consistent ways, doing the same sorts of things in the same order at the same time of day, day in and day out.

When you misplace something, imagine what you usually do, where you usually walk, or where you generally write things down. In most cases, you won't have to search far outside your normal routines to locate lost items or information.

I advise people to look in the usual areas, but to look *higher* and *lower* than usual. Things are commonly mislaid on shelves *above* the desk or *under* the counter, if they are not in their usual places *on* the desk or counter.

Retrace Your Steps

You are sitting behind your desk busily involved in a project. Suddenly, you think of something that you need. You get out of your chair and walk over to your secretary. When you reach his or her desk, you have forgotten what you needed. After an embarrassing moment or two, you return to your desk and the thought usually returns right away.

Most persons discover for themselves that returning to where they thought of something can help recapture the lost memory. This technique can also be extended to more general situations and contexts. You dream up a new angle on one of your projects while in the elevator returning from lunch. When you reach your office, you have forgotten what your thought was. Go back to the elevator and ride it up and down a few times. Ride up the same floors and stand in the same spot in the elevator. This may trigger the same thoughts again. The more closely you duplicate what you were doing at the time of your thought, the more successful you will be in recapturing the lost memory.

> Constance W., a private secretary, applied this principle when she had difficulty transcribing a sentence from her shorthand notes. She took her notebook into the office and sat on the chair where she had taken the dictation. Still she could not decipher the sentence. Then, without leaving the chair, she . . . . began to move her writing hand as if she were taking down the preceding paragraph—warming up to the puzzling sentence. As soon as her hand came to the troublesome notes, she recalled the correct meaning in a flash (Donald and Elanor Laird, *Techniques for Efficient Remembering*).

This same technique can also be used to recapture a mental thread. During a conversation, we occasionally get sidetracked onto a tangent and are unable to remember the important point that we were driving at. "Now, where was I heading?" we sheepishly ask the other person. Recapture the original idea by tracing backward through your sequence of thoughts. Instead of walking back into the physical setting in which you had the thought, mentally step back through your mind.

Develop a Stock Way around Temporary Name Loss

From time to time, we are caught by surprise by an old acquaintance and cannot think of his or her name unless given a bit of time. The worse thing to do is to stand awkwardly facing the individual, stammering and apologizing for your poor memory. This makes for an uncomfortable situation for both of you, and your increased embarrassment almost ensures that the other person's name will not come back to you. Consider using one of the following techniques to help you out in these tight situations.

One graceful procedure is to offer your name as a trade. If you are Samuel Gordon, march boldly up to the person and say, "Sam Gordon here . . . nice to see you again!" Many people will reciprocate by giving their names back to you. This forceful approach avoids the awkwardness of stumbling for a name, and it also gives the other person an "out" if he or she has forgotten *your* name. With this technique, the other person may not even notice that you could not remember his or her name.

Another technique is the temporary conversational diversion. Look at the person for a moment and then say, "I didn't recognize you at first. How have you been? Have you changed something?" This will usually lead into discussion of the individual's recent experiences, and the awkward uncertainty about the name will be avoided. Compliment the person on his or her hairstyle, suit, suntan, or distinctive piece of jewelry: "That is certainly a nice shirt you have on today! Where did you pick it up?" Another tactic is to say something like, "Boy, it's been a long time. When was the last time we saw [talked] to each other?"

All these approaches are cordial, but the focus is thrown on another topic, which gives you a way to avoid the name for a moment, and provide some time for your memory to search for the missing information. Furthermore, you may pick up a relevant clue during the conversation that will trigger the person's name.

Some auditory persons have difficulty recalling a name until they can hear the person's voice again. If you experience this, take the offensive and greet the person from a distance with a standard salutation: "What's up with you?" or "Where have you been?" Hopefully, they will give a response which will jog the name in your memory.

> A prominent British publisher met a woman he knew in the posh members' lounge at Ascot. But he couldn't place her—neither her name nor who she was. They began to chat—*she* knew *him*. He was desperately looking for a clue to her identity. Finally, she mentioned her sister. Aha! he thought. "Your sister," he said, "what's she doing these days?" She stared at him for a moment, and then said, "Oh, she's still queen."

Activate Your Senses

If you have some information that you are blocking on, warm up to it by activating your senses. It is difficult for visual persons to think and remember if they have their eyes closed. Watch their eyes dart around as they recall an old friend or think about the party last weekend. Auditory types cannot easily think or remember while being quiet. Hearing themselves helps to recall or relive an event. And motion-oriented individuals need body movement and action to think, solve problems, and remember most efficiently. They will pace and gyrate as they try to pull up the information.

If you are auditory, talk aloud about the information, event, person, or meeting. For visualizers, glance around at the walls, floor, and ceiling—even out the window. Keep the eyes moving. If you are motion-centered, walk around the room, down the hall, or step through the type of movements which you experienced at the time.

Free-Associate

In some situations, you have the luxury of taking your time in retrieving information. Let's say you hid your favorite hunting rifle before your trip to the Bahamas. You come back home and cannot remember where you put it. Try free association. Recall all the details of preparing for your pleasure trip. Don't worry that the details may or may not be related to the key information you are seeking. Simply keep pulling out all your recollections in an unforced and unconstrained manner. As you continue with your recall, you are mentally reconstructing the experience with all its accompanying cues and memory hooks. The summation of all the information at once may help resurrect the lost item. Or it may be associated with a piece of information that you did not suspect at all.

Try Repeated Recalls

This memory-jogging procedure is similar to the one above, except that it is used for *lists* of items. You attended a meeting with seven keys to better people management. Despite a valiant attempt to remember all seven points, the next day you can recall only five.

Try recalling the list over and over again, five or six times. Give yourself a few minutes to an hour between recalls. You may recall the information differently each time, adding some new items and dropping some old items. Therefore, write down each recall effort and don't throw away your old recall sheets. This will provide protection against dropping some items.

Warm Up to Big Memory Jobs

Recalling information from long-term memory is not instantaneous. It takes about one second for most pieces of information to be pulled out of long-term memory after given the proper cue. For more complex ideas or concepts, it may take several seconds. When dealing with a large amount of information, it may take much longer to recall numerous details and integrate them into a comprehensive picture. If I asked you to consider the consequences of a nuclear war, or the selection of a new phone system for your office, these evaluations would involve a lengthy recall task.

Most important decisions or problems require that a large amount of information be simultaneously evaluated and compared. In a fast-paced business, it does not pay to sit on decisions too long, or develop "ponderitis" while the competition beats your socks off. But it does take a few minutes of devoted effort to adequately recall and evaluate the issues so that the best decision can be made.

Devote several minutes to recalling all you know about a topic before making a decision. The shoot-from-the-hip executive may be admired for his or her apparent boldness and quick thinking, but such a person has probably failed to consider some factors in the decision, because memory recall doesn't work that rapidly.

Sleep on It

Occasionally, people encounter a situation where they have a difficult time figuring out a solution to a problem or making an appropriate decision. Some informal evidence exists that your memory can work toward a solution on its own as you rest. Therefore, in these cases try the following technique. Just before retiring for the night, briefly review all the facets of the problem, or the issues involved in the decision. Talk to yourself, specifically outlining what type of solution or answer you desire. Then go to sleep. Be sure to have a tablet of paper and a pencil beside your bed so that if you wake up with the solution, you can write it down.

If this procedure does not work the first time, give it another chance or two. Although sleep is the best time for it, you can also try it during other "off times" where heavy mental activity is not required: driving home from work, commuting on the train, attending the symphony, jogging, or sitting in the spa. Try priming your memory just before these activities, and then let it go.

MEMOREVIEW: Jogging Your Memory

Do Not Panic: Emotions will block your recall.
Focus Away: Switch your attention from the blocked item.
Back Off from a Wrong Guess: Start again from the top.
Search Each Memory File Drawer: Look through different areas.
Go through the Alphabet: Search from A to Z until you find it.
Be Logical: Recall your usual behaviors.
Retrace Your Steps: Get back to the starting point.
Develop a Stock Way around Temporary Name Loss: Don't hedge.
Activate Your Senses: Warm up your sensory pathways.
Free-Associate: Let your memory wander on its own.
Try Repeated Recalls: Recall it over and over, again.
Warm Up to Big Memory Jobs: Don't decide from the hip.
Sleep on It: Allow your brain's downtime to work for you.

24

Making It Work

If you have gotten this far in the book, you are serious about changing the way you manage your memory. I hope you have already tried some of the suggestions and experienced some clear improvement in your ability to remember information. But in order to make the changes become a *permanent* reality of your day-to-day activities, you need time.

As with all other areas of behavior change, there are no quick "fixes." In order to lose weight or stop smoking, there needs to be a long-term commitment to change. The same is true for memory improvement.

Becoming more proficient in memory management involves four basic ingredients:

1. A long-term goal
2. A series of short-term goals to get there
3. A way to monitor your improvement
4. Techniques to accentuate your progress

Other memory books are filled with stories about allegedly real people who acquired enormous riches and respect as a result of improved memory skills. I'm sure that the authors mean well by telling these stories. They want to motivate their readers toward the goal of a perfect memory. But this approach discourages more readers than it encourages. Most people want a *better* memory, not a *perfect* one.

People are generally intimidated by such stories, especially in light of the slow improvement which they may experience. Readers become embarrassed or discouraged when it becomes apparent that their own memory powers will not reach the level suggested by the authors. The reality is that those individuals who exhibit truly exceptional memories have spent an enormous amount of time, over a number of years, working to improve their skills.

In this chapter, I will provide a practical approach to habit change, with realistic expectations. People may vary considerably in their innate memory capacity, but everyone can experience substantial improvement through a focused application of the principles presented in this book.

Get Your Overall Goal Clearly in Mind

In order to implement the memory changes you desire, determine exactly *what* you want to improve. Perhaps the following questions will help:

1. In what areas has your memory let you down: with names, numbers, appointments, conversations, reading material, meetings?
2. In what situations has difficulty with remembering information caused you embarrassment or wasted time?
3. Do people accuse you of forgetfulness, in jest or otherwise? If so, what does your "forgetfulness" involve?
4. What are your long-range career or personal goals, and how can a well-managed memory help you get there?
5. Is there a person whose memory abilities you would like to emulate?

Think through a typical business day and list the items for which your memory could use improvement: the place your car is parked in the garage, the names of clients to call and in what order, or information contained in business articles.

Students in school are prepared to learn and absorb almost anything that is presented to them. That is their task through the early years of life, and few children question the necessity of learning for its own sake. Adults, however, are much more pragmatic. They find information not directly related to their lives difficult to

Making It Work

absorb. But information that is clearly applicable and immediately beneficial is easy for adults to deal with.

At the end of this chapter, there are several memory management worksheets to help you with goal setting. For the topic area(s) which you have targeted for improvement, select one or two suggestions under each of the four sections (Attend, Associate, Rehearse, Support), referring back to the Memoreview at the end of each chapter.

Give Yourself Plenty of Time

The hardest point in changing your habits is at the start. Altering any long-established routine is most difficult at first, and becomes easier later. At the beginning, you are working against old memory tendencies, and the immediate benefit may be small during this initial, gradual improvement. But as you increase your memory management ability, the rewards will become clearer in terms of less wasted time, increased self-confidence, and compliments from others. Stretch out your vision for memory enhancement over months, rather than days.

Make Some Intermediate Goals and Monitor Your Progress

The long trip toward your overall goal can be made easier by breaking it down into smaller stages. When your accomplishments are very specific, your progress will be evident.

Suppose that you wanted to increase your name memory at professional meetings. Start off with a preliminary assessment. How many new names do you typically remember after such a gathering? Set your goal for the next meeting at a modest increase of several additional persons. Don't try to set your goal so high that you are bound to fail. The next meeting after that, increase your goal by a few more people. If you don't achieve your mark, set your goal a bit lower. Keep a continual record of your progress so that you can see your improvement.

When your trouble is with numbers, set a goal to memorize three new numbers each day during the first week. If you achieve this goal and feel comfortable with your progress, set your next goal at five numbers a day. The meaning or value of the individual numbers is not as important as the practice in attacking and memorizing them.

Don't Tell Anyone That You Are Improving Your Memory

For some perverse reason, the average person is full of bad jokes about memory and memory failure. People also take delight in testing you when they discover that you are becoming a memory "expert." Although this is good-natured chiding, it could be discouraging if you are just starting to improve your memory skills. Your developing abilities and confidence can be dealt a blow by these offhand remarks.

One of the harsh realities about memory performance is that your lapses are immediately evident to others. If you claim that you are changing your eating or smoking habits, any backsliding may not be immediately obvious. In contrast, when your memory fails on a name, fact, or phone number, it is often in front of witnesses.

The best approach is to make your work on memory improvement your secret. Keep track of your progress and let that be your reward. Others will soon take notice of your improved ability and add their own compliments. If you need social support in your efforts, find a memory improvement partner. Recruit someone else who also has a desire to improve his or her memory skills, and share your successes on a regular basis.

Become Friends with Your Memory and Trust It

Too often, an adversarial relationship evolves between a person and his or her memory. The memory bears the brunt of a host of irritations engendered by a lack of performance *on demand*. Irritation then changes into distrust. The partnership between person and mental ability dissolves. We sometimes deal with other body parts in a similar manner: "My stomach is killing me" should actually be "I have abused my stomach and it is telling me so." This way of imaging a body part as a separate and combatitive entity not only is inaccurate, but avoids confronting the inadequacies of our own behaviors.

This negative relationship with your memory can cause unnecessary memory failure and prevent progress. Trust your memory the way you trust a friend. If it lets you down, you will gain more by accepting it and trying again than from chastising it and reinforcing distrust.

Create a Hedge against Memory Failure

One of the added burdens of a memory failure is monetary loss: the umbrella that you lost because you left it in the restaurant, the bill that you forget to pay and get a late charge for, or the appointment that you missed, which caused the loss of a contract. Keep track of, or set aside, some funds to cover these incidents. Be sure that you record your real or potential losses. If you allow a certain, reasonable amount of money for these memory difficulties, they will be less traumatic. Keep a document of these expenses, so that you can witness the shrinkage as your memory improves.

Record the Positive Results from Improved Memory Management

On the following page is a space to record the good things that happen to you as a result of improved memory management. Whenever someone compliments you on remembering something, record it. If you impress a client by quickly recalling some business facts or numbers, write that down. When you remember all the items in a shopping list for the first time, record that.

We tend to overlook our successes when we become temporarily discouraged. This list will help prevent this from occurring. Keep your progress in focus and your motivation up.

Positive Experiences from Improved Memory Management

EXPERIENCE	EVENT	DATE

MEMOREVIEW: Making It Work

Get your overall goal clearly in mind.
Give yourself plenty of time.
Make some intermediate goals and monitor your progress.
Don't tell anyone that you are improving your memory.
Become friends with your memory and trust it.
Create a hedge against memory failure.
Record the positive results from improved memory management.

MEMORY MANAGEMENT WORKSHEET

	ATTEND	ASSOCIATE	REHEARSE	SUPPORT
NAMES				
PERSONAL INFORMATION				
CONVERSATIONS				
READING MATERIAL				
MEETINGS				

Memory management worksheet for Chapters 8 to 12

MEMORY MANAGEMENT WORKSHEET

	ATTEND	ASSOCIATE	REHEARSE	SUPPORT
TASKS TO ACCOMPLISH				
TASKS COMPLETED				
NUMBERS				
MAKING A SPEECH				
EXAMINATIONS				

Memory management worksheet for Chapters 14 to 18

Index

Acronyms, 41, 79, 190, 219–220
Aging, 10
Alarms, 146
Answering machine, 149, 150
Anxiety, 66, 183, 185, 233–234
Appointment book, 56, 151–152
Attention, 27–36
  audiences, 214–217
  conversations, 96–99
  examinations, 187–188
  from others, 8
  meetings, 118–120
  memos, 224–226
  messages, 207–208
  names, 67–74
  numbers, 165–167
  personal information, 88–90
  reading material, 105–109
  tasks
    completed, 154–155
    to accomplish, 137–138
  wandering, 27–28, 33, 108, 117, 154
Arrivals, 32, 73, 118, 184
Association, 32–43
  audiences, 218–221
  auditory, 40–41
  conversations, 99–101
  examinations, 188–190
  kinesthetic, 41–42
  meetings, 120–123
  memos, 226–228
  messages, 208–210
  names, 74–80
  numbers, 167–174
  personal information, 90–91
  reading material, 109–113
  speeches, 181–183
  tasks
    completed, 156–158
    to accomplish, 138–142
  visual, 38–39
Attitude, 117, 165–166, 246–247
Audience, 213–222

Body
  parts, 130, 182
  postures, 182

Calculator, 173–174
Calendar, 142, 151–152
Card
  business, 74, 82–83, 85, 93, 205
  cue, 192
  file, 57, 93, 102, 124–125
  note, 56–57, 149

253

Competition, 30–31, 120
Completing tasks, 7, 35, 96, 118
Computer, 102–103, 146, 226
Concentration, 108
Conversations, 95–104
Copying, 114
cost–benefit analysis, 31–32
Cueing
   alphabetical, 236
   cards, 184, 192
   objects, 139

Daydreaming, 12, 33
Departures, 82, 92, 102, 123–124
Diagrams/charts, 41, 121, 167–168, 227–228
Diaries, 159
Discussion partner, 47, 81, 112, 113, 120, 124, 148, 191–192
Distractions, 12, 27, 33–34, 67–69, 96–97, 99, 118, 201,
Drugs, 9, 189
Dry run, 184

Energy level, 32, 105–106, 119
Environment
   external, 6–7, 48–49, 97, 106–107, 139, 188–189
   internal, 9, 189
Examinations, 186–195
Eye contact, 200

Face, 71–72, 96–97
Free association, 240
Follow up, 206, 211
Forgetting, 3–10
   physical causes, 9–10
   psychological causes, 3–8

Goal setting, 107, 243–246
Goodbyes, 82, 92
Greetings, 88–89, 225

Habits
   changing, 25–26, 243–249
   distracting, 68–69, 214–215
   inattention, 28, 32, 108
Hiding places, 161
Hobbies, 89, 172
Hurrying, 154

Indexes, 115
Information
   limits, 13, 14, 34–35, 42, 73, 95, 102, 137, 155, 227
   passive, 43
   personal, 87–99
Interference, 42, 66, 114–115, 201
Interruptions, 95, 97, 207
Introductions, 67–68, 81, 83–84, 199–206

Jogging memory, 233–242
Jokes, 217

Key words, 189

Lists, 56, 127–136, 183, 190
   borrowing
   chain, 112, 127, 128, 134
   check, 160
   lending, 161–162
   location, 127, 129–130, 135, 181–182
   names, 83–84
   pegword, 127, 131–134, 135, 141–142
   permanent, 150

Main points (extracting), 98, 166, 189
Magnetic letters, 151
Messages, 207–212

Index

Memos, 223-230
Meetings 117-126
Mental images
 auditory, 19-20, 40-41, 75, 91, 100-101, 112, 121, 131-133, 139-140, 157, 169
 motion, 20-21, 77-78, 91, 112-113, 121-122, 123, 140-141, 157-158, 172-173, 182-183
 visual, 18-19, 39, 74-75, 90-91, 100, 110, 121, 122-123, 133-134, 139, 141-142, 156, 167-168, 181-182
Memoreview
 audience, 222
 conversations, 104
 examinations, 195
 introducing yourself, 206
 jogging, 242
 making it work, 249
 meetings, 126
 memos, 230
 messages, 212
 names, 86
 numbers, 179
 personal information, 94
 reading material, 116
 speeches, 185
 tasks
  completed, 163
  to accomplish, 152
Memory
 blocks, 5, 193-194, 233-242
 long-term, 3, 11, 14
 sensory, 11, 12
 short-term, 11, 13
 styles, 15-24, 208-209, 226, 239
  auditory, 19-20, 226
  motion, 20-21, 226
  test, 15-17, 22
  visual, 18-19, 226
Mnemonic techniques
 chain, 112, 127, 128, 134
 locations, 127, 129-130, 135, 181-182

 number, 175-178
 pegword, 127, 131-134, 135, 141-142
Monetary loss, 247
Motivation, 31, 187
Movement, 72, 101, 140, 157-158

Name tags, 74, 203-204
Names, 65-85
Noise, 157, 188
Note
 cards, 56-57, 149
 pads, 150
 sticky, 150
Numbers, 164-179
 fear, 165-166
 mnemonic technique, 175-178
 telephone, 167-168, 169, 172-173, 174

Occupations, 90-91, 201-202, 203
Outlines, 109, 180
Overlearning, 50, 183

Pacing activities, 158, 208
Pantomime, 140
Paraphrasing, 48
Participation, 41, 227
Personalizing, 29-30, 123, 170-171, 172, 209-210
Photographs
 mental, 90, 110
 real, 82
Postures, 72, 182
Preparation, 32, 83-84, 92, 137-138, 228-229
Possessions
 labelling, 162
 misplacing, 160-161, 236-237

Questioning
  others, 97–98, 121, 192, 204, 227
  yourself, 47, 113–114, 191

Reading material, 105–116
Reflection times, 46–47, 81, 83, 143–144, 155, 158–159
Rehearsal, 44–51
  audiences, 221
  conversations, 101–102
  examinations, 190–192
  meetings, 123–124
  memos, 228
  messages, 210–211
  names, 80–83
  personal information, 92
  reading material, 113–114
  spacing out, 45–46
  speeches, 183–184
  tasks
    completed, 158–159
    to accomplish, 143–144
Repetition, 47, 49, 69, 80, 100–102, 112, 190–191, 204, 210, 228, 240
Reminders
  auditory, 147
  checklist, 149–152
  people, 57, 84, 147–149
  physical, 145–146
  related, 54–55, 144
  unrelated, 55–56, 144–146
  visual, 145
Retracing steps
  mentally, 236–237, 238
  physically, 237
Rewards, 107, 247–249
Rhymes, 76–77, 169

Self-consciousness, 33, 67–68
Self-talk, 32–33, 139–140, 157
Skimming, 110, 194

Sleep, 193, 241
Small talk, 71
Special favors, 147–148
Speeches, 180–185
Speed reading, 110
Stories, 77, 91
Stress, 5–6, 50, 65–66, 164, 183, 193–194, 215, 233
Successes, 247–249
Summary, 109, 114, 211, 228–229
Support, 52–59
  audiences, 222
  conversations, 102–103
  examinations, 193–194
  meetings, 124–125
  memos, 229
  messages, 211
  names, 83–85
  personal information, 93–94
  reading material, 114–115
  speeches, 184–185
  tasks
    completed, 160–162
    to accomplish, 144–152

Tape recorders, 49, 103, 124, 149
Tasks
  completed, 153–163
  future, 137–152
  unexpected, 138
Telephone
  answering machine, 149, 150
  conversations, 95, 97, 101, 148, 207
  number associations, 167–168, 169, 172–173, 174
Thinking ahead, 98–99
Time images, 141–142

Underlining, 108, 111, 191–192

Index

Vocal patterning, 40, 72, 75, 76, 112, 169, 200–201

Warming up, 106, 166, 240–241
Writing, 41, 99–100, 111, 122, 190–191, 210